IT AIN'T SO!

SHOELESS JOE JACKSON'S STORY

A Play in Two Acts

And Afterword

By

Alan Thurston

Cover Photo: 1916 Shoeless Joe Jackson (Alamy Stoc Photos)

Author Photo: Pablo Minier photographer

Cast of Characters

Shoeless Joe Jackson   *Baseball Star*

Katie Jackson   *Joe's Wife*

Ring Lardner   *Baseball Writer*

Charles Comiskey   *White Sox Owner*

Harry Grey   *Team Secretary*

Kid Gleason   *White Sox Manager*

Chick Gandil   *White Sox First Baseman*

Lefty Williams   *White Sox Pitcher*

Swede Risberg   *White Sox Shortstop*

Sleepy Billy   *A Gambler*

Ty Cobb   *Baseball Star*

Connie Mack   *Manager of the A's*

Tommie Stouch   *Baseball Scout*

A Boy, an Umpire Priest, Judge, Prosecutor, Fans and Reporters.

The play is a dramatic depiction of the rise and fall of one of baseball's greats, Shoeless Joe Jackson, who played in the Major Leagues from 1908 until his banishment from organized baseball in 1920 because of his alleged involvement in the Black Sox Scandal.

SCENE

Various locations from the life of Joe Jackson.

TIME

Between 1908 – 1920.

NOTE: There are many speaking parts in the play with several roles consisting of very few lines. In my opinion, the play can be performed with 12 actors including some doubling.

NOTE ABOUT THE SET: Little scenery is required as two or three tables, some chairs and a few benches representing baseball stands are all the furniture needed.

NOTE ABOUT THE SONGS: I have included short excerpts of public domain songs from the era that are to be spoken, not sung.

NOTE: The article read by Ring at the end of the play was written by Hugh Fullerton.

<u>SONGS</u> (Short excerpts of public domain songs that are to be spoken not sung.)

ACT 1	ACT 2
Sweet Rosie O'Grady	Lazy Mary Will Ya Get Up?
Take Me Out to the Ballgame	Gambling Man
Gambling Man	Budweiser's a Friend of Mine
America Here's My Boy	Old Black Joe

For my brother, Bob, who told me many years ago, that he thought the story of Shoeless Joe Jackson would make a good play. It is my sincere hope that I have proven him to have been right.

<u>ACT 1</u>

SETTING: Cotton mill town near Greenville, SC.

AT RISE: In the black, low-tonal dramatic

music is heard. As characters from

JOE'S life deliver a line, a LIGHT

SPECIAL is brought up on them.

These lines grow rhythmically to a

crescendo to JOE'S light coming up

on him DS.

COMISKEY: Here's a blank check. Find out how much
they want and fill in the figure yourself.

COBB: If you wanna be a great hitter like me, you gotta
be real scientific about it.

1

SLEEPY BILLY: C'mon, it'll make the game mor intrestin'.

LEFTY: Take it, Joe!

KATIE: Y'er a hero just like the great Gilgamesh!

RING: You like Comiskey Park franks?

CHICK: Sleep on it, Joe.

GREY: You're involved.

BOY: I wanna be a great hitter just like you!

JOE: Maybe bein' able to hit a ball harder'n it's eve been hit before ain't no kinda blessin'. Way I see it…It' a curse.

(Baseball writer, RING LARDNEI

carrying a notepad, crosses DS.)

RING: Joe Jackson, a poor country boy who made good, climbing the heights of fame and glory.

(The BOY flips JOE a baseball glove.)

BOY: C'mon, Joey, ya gotta get goin'! Today's the big day! Y'er gonna play in front of Tommie Stouch!

JOE: Who's he?

BOY: Who's he? Only the top scout for Connie Mack hisself, that's who. And he's comin' here special just to see you!

JOE: He's comin' all this way jus' to see me? Damn!

(Two FANS and an OLD MAN enter. The BOY crosses to the OLD MAN who is holding an object wrapped in a cotton cloth.)

3

FANS: We're with ya, Joey!

RING: Joe started working in the cotton mills near Greenville, South Carolina when he was six. He'd work 12 hours a day but would play ball whenever he could. Back in those days, the mill owners formed ball teams to keep their workers happy. And Joe picked up the game fast...*real* fast.

FAN 1: First he was a catcher...

FAN 2: Till his mama made him stop.

FAN 1: Then he was a pitcher...

FAN 2: Till he broke a fella's arm.

FAN 1: Then he switched to the outfield...

FAN 2: Where he fit in real natural like.

(FAN 1 flips JOE a ball. He throws as the crowd "oohs and ahs." JOE'S brother, DAVEY, who walks with a crutch, enters and crosses to JOE.)

DAVEY: Mama says it's OK for me to watch the game today, Joey. Wish I could play with ya.

JOE: Sure wish ya could, too, Davey. The bosses never shoulda let ya near them damn machines in the mill.

DAVEY: Ya know how them bosses are.

JOE: Sons of bitches.

DAVEY: Ya gotta try'n get outta here before they cripple ya, too.

JOE: If'n I keep breathin' that durn air in the mill, I won't have wind enough to play ball, that's fer sure.

5

(The OLD MAN, holding his

object, crosses to JOE.)

OLD MAN: Hey, Joey, I made ya a present.

(JOE does not hear. The

OLD MAN unwraps the

object, revealing a black

bat.)

I made it special just for ya.

(JOE slowly takes the bat. He

tests its weight and swings.)

I hope ya like it.

JOE: Don't know how to thank ya, sir.

OLD MAN: Hittin' a homer'll be plenty thanks for me.

FAN 1: Just roun' the corner…

FAN 2: From where I now reside.

FAN 1: Lives the cutest little girl…

FAN 2: That ever I done spied.

> *(A young girl, KATIE, enters and*
> *crosses to JOE as he hides the*
> *bat behind his back.)*

KATIE: What ya got there, Joey?

JOE: Katie…I'm in love.

KATIE: Ya are, are ya, Joey!?

JOE: Yes, I am. And she's 'bout the prettiest durn thing
I ever seen in my life.

KATIE: Joey, stop! Y'er makin' me blush!

JOE: Yep, it was love at first sight. Her name's…Betsy

KATIE: *(Disappointed.)* Betsy!?...Oh.

JOE: (*Laughs as he shows her the bat.)*   Katie, meet m
beautiful Black Betsy. Betsy, meet my darlin' Katie.

FAN 1: No bat better than Black Betsy!

FAN 2: No bat better than Black Betsy!

FAN 1: You can search the whole world roun'.

FAN 2: I swear it never will be found.

BOTH: No bat better than Black Betsy!

UMPIRE: Play ball!

KATIE: Carry my hairpin, will ya, Joey, it'll bring ya good luck!

(JOE smiles as he puts the hairpin in his pocket and kicks off his shoes.)

Ya gonna play with yer shoes off, Joey?

JOE: Have to, honey. These new spikes raisin' blisters somethin' terrible. Besides, I gits better toeholds without 'em.

RING: *(Writes in his notebook.)* Plays ball in his stocking feet! Shoeless Joe! It sings!

(TOMMIE STOUCH enters.)

Tommie Stouch. Top baseball scout for the great Connie Mack, manager of the Philadelphia A's.

(RING crosses to STOUCH.)

What brings ya to Greenville, Tommie?

STOUCH: Heard about this here hick who some folks'er thinkin's the new Ty Cobb.

9

RING: Ty Cobb?!

STOUCH: Yeah, but I've heard that one before. They say he can hit the ball harder than any mortal man. Mind ya, though, I'm kinda skeptical.

(JOE swings. A loud crack

of the bat is heard.)

RING: Still skeptical?

STOUCH: Did you hear the crack of that bat?   Music to my ears!

(STOUCH crosses to JOE.)

Say, Joe, ya 'spect to be playin' for mill teams the rest of your life?

JOE: Sure hope not, sir.   I'm wantin' to get outta them mills soon's I can.

STOUCH: I'd like ya to come with me on the next train to Philadelphia.   10

JOE: Philadelphia?

STOUCH: That's right. After all, the A's play half their games in Philly.

JOE: That'd sure be great, Mr. Stouch! I'd love to play for the A's and the great Connie Mack! But…

STOUCH: But what?

JOE: It's jus'…I gotta check with someone first.

STOUCH: Do yer checkin', Joe, but remember Mr. Mack can't be kept waitin'.

> *(BLACKOUT. LIGHTS UP on JOE and KATIE sitting on a park bench.)*

JOE: D'ya think you'd like bein' married to a pro-fesh-i-on-al ballplayer?

11

KATIE: Married? It wouldn't matter to me what ya did, but I'm only 15. I don't think I'm ready to get married yet, Joey.

JOE: Fifteen's old enough. Look at Rosie Jenkins. She's got two kids already and she's only 14.

KATIE: Yeah, but look at 'er! She looks like she's at least 18. Marriage sure does age a gal.

JOE: Thought ya liked me, Katie.

KATIE: Ya know I do, Joey, but I can't get married yet. Like my mama says, once y'er married y'er stuck for life. And I sure don' wanna get stuck here. Look at this place. Dreary shacks. People workin' all day in the mill, gettin' sick breathin' that lousy air even crippled from the machines like Davey. It just ain't right.

JOE: What ain't right?

KATIE: Way we do all the work and them bosses make all the money.   12

JOE: Damn right it ain't right.

KATIE: Boss rides in here in his fancy car…

JOE: …rides out with a suitcase full of dough.

KATIE: He don't breathe the air…

JOE: …or stay long enough to get the sound of the machines stuck in his head.

KATIE: My daddy wakes up in the middle of the night screamin' 'cause he can't stop hearin' that noise.

JOE: That's why I play ball…To get me away from it all. When I'm on the field, don't think 'bout nuttin' but the ball. It's jus' me'n the ball. Almos' like the ball's a person…got a life of its own. Don't think 'bout the machines or the bad air or the racket. It's on the ball field …Where I can breathe free.

KATIE: But what 'bout when ya can't play no more? There's no future for us here.   13

JOE: Not here fer sure, Katie, but there'll be a future fe
us somewhere better'n this. And we'll be the ones callir
the shots just like them bosses in their fancy cars.

KATIE: But there's so much I wanna do before I settle
down. So many places I gotta see.

JOE: That's why we're made for each other, darlin'. A
the wife of a pro-fesh-i-on-al ballplayer, you can trave
all over the country. We'll be rich'n I'll buy ya nic
clothes and a big house.

KATIE: How 'bout a brand-new automobile like thos
highfalutin' Clarks in Greenville!

VOICE: ALL ABOARD!

(STOUCH enters.)

STOUCH: Come on, Joe, the train's a leavin'!

KATIE: Ya better git along then, Joey.   1

JOE: So, ya gonna marry me? I ain't gonna leave fer nowhere till ya give me yer answer.

KATIE: Durn it, Joey, course I will. Y'er the only one fer me.

> *(JOE kisses KATIE, who exits.*
> *JOE joins STOUCH in two chairs*
> *at CS. A train is heard as two*
> *FANS enter.)*

FAN 1: Don't go up North there, Joe.

FAN 2: Don't go up North there, Joe.

FAN 1: They may smile, but don't mean a thing.

FAN 2: They'll make you feel like y'er a king.

BOTH: Don't go up North there, Joe.

> *(The FANS exit.)*

JOE: Don't know if I'm doin' the right thing. Got this awful feelin' in the pit of my stomach. Like I mightn't fit in there up North.

STOUCH: It's gonna be great, Joe!

JOE: Ain't never been outside the South. All those people up there scurryin' around like ants.

STOUCH: I don't understand ya, Joe. Y'er gonna be a Major Leaguer! What more could anyone want in America? Even President Taft said he'd rather play ball than be in the White House.

JOE: But...

STOUCH: Relax, Joe, we'll talk about it in the morning. Right now, I gotta get me some shut-eye.

(STOUCH goes to sleep.)

VOICE: Next stop Charlotte!   16

(JOE jumps the train. He crosses DR to the entering KATIE as CONNIE MACK enters.)

MACK: So, where is he?

STOUCH: I'm sorry, Mr. Mack. He must've slipped off the train while I was sleepin'.

MACK: You go back and fetch him. Tell him to report at once or he can forget about being a professional ballplayer North, South or anywhere.

(MACK and STOUCH exit.)

KATIE: Go back, Joe. Give it a chance. Maybe things will be different from what ya been thinking.

JOE: It's a whole different world up there, Katie. They ain't like us'ns.

KATIE: But that's where the money is, Joey. We'll never get rich if ya stay down here.   17

JOE: That's the only thing gonna get me to go up there.

KATIE: What?

JOE: Money, Katie, the money. I'll make my pile, then I'll head on back home.

KATIE: And we're gonna have a big house. Biggest anyone ever seen!

(STOUCH enters and crosses to JOE)

STOUCH: C'mon, Joe! You're a lucky bastard 'cause Mr. Mack's willin' to give ya another chance. He could've had ya blacklisted, ya know.

JOE: Blacklisted?

STOUCH: That's right. Banned from baseball for life. So, if ya ever hope to play ball anywhere, you'd better come with me and you'd better hurry 'bout it.   18

KATIE: Go with him, Joey…I'll join ya as soon as I can.

JOE: That a promise?

KATIE: It's a promise.

> *(JOE kisses KATIE, then picks*
> *up Black Betsy as KATIE and*
> *STOUCH exit. RING enters.)*

RING: Joe's reputation as the new Ty Cobb preceded him. In those days, rookies were by no means welcome. They were considered a threat to veteran players who were afraid of losing their jobs.

> *(RING exits as JOE crosses to*
> *CS where he is met by 2 VETS*
> *who push him from one to the*
> *other.)*

VET 1: Well, well, will ya look who's here! It's the new rookie phenom hisself.

VET 2: We bin waitin' on ya. Nice of ya to finally show up.

VET 1: Guess he jus' wanted to make a gran' entrance or somethin'.

VET 2: Say, Rube, is it true ya can't even write yer name?

VET 1: Don't pick on the poor hillbilly. Ya know how ignorant them boys are.

> *(VET 2 puts his hat on sideways*
> *and sticks his finger in his nose.*

VET 2: Look at me, I'm a hillbilly! Oh shit, I can't get my finger outta my nose, it's stuck. Won't somebody please help me?

VET 1: Hillbillies got no time fer book learnin'. They're too busy screwin' their pigs.

VET 2: Say, boy, ya ever screw a pig?

JOE: Maybe...What's yer wife look like?

> *(VET 2 grabs Betsy and starts to smash the bat. JOE snatches the bat back as the VETS laugh and exit as MACK enters.)*

JOE: Wish I'd never come up here.

MACK: Do you mean that, Joe? Don't pay those boys any mind. I expect they'll shut up once they see you hit a baseball.

JOE: I don't know if I can play up here, Mr. Mack. What with me bein' homesick and those bastards...'Scuse me.

21

MACK: That's all right. Though I don't like cussin' myself, I do have to admit they can be bastards. Don't take them seriously. They'll never let up if they think they're gettin' your goat.

JOE: They'll never let up s'long's I can't...

MACK: So long as you can't what?

JOE: S'long's I can't...read.

MACK: If you want to learn, I'll be happy to get someone to teach you.

JOE: No! Sorry...I mean...not now.

MACK: Why?

JOE: Well, Mr. Mack, what if I ain't able to learn?

(MACK exits as 2 VETS enter.) 22

VOICE: Now batting for the Philadelphia A's, Shoeless Joe Jackson!

> *(One of the VETS winds up and throws. JOE swings and falls to one knee as RING enters.)*

VOICE: Strike one!

VET 1: *(Laughs.)* Look at that hayseed!

RING: Say, Joe! Whaddya think of the trade?

JOE: Trade? What trade?

RING: Haven't you heard? Connie Mack's sending you to another team. Says it's for your own good.

JOE: Where?

VOICE: Now batting for the Cleveland Naps, Shoeless Joe Jackson!

> *(The VET winds up and throws. JOE again swings and misses.)*

VOICE: Strike Two!

VET 2: Hey Jackson! Can ya spell "cat"?

> *(JOE swings at a third pitch. A loud crack of the bat is heard as the VETS watch the flight of the ball.)*

JOE: Yeah. Can y'all spell "shit"?

> *(The VETS exit.)*

RING: I can make ya a rich man, Joe.

JOE: How ya figure on doin' that? Y'er jus' a baseball writer.

RING: I'm more than a writer.

JOE: Y'are?

RING: That's right. I'm also a myth maker.

JOE: A myth maker? What'n damnation's a myth maker?

RING: There's a lot of power in this here pen of mine, Joe. It can make or break careers.

JOE: That a fact?

RING: The masses need myths to make it through their miserable lives.

JOE: How 'xactly's yer myth makin' gonna make me money?   25

RING: My stories about Shoeless Joe will put backside in the seats. The owners pay those players who make them wealthy.

JOE: Seems kinda dishonest to me. The truth…

RING: Some say the truth don't mean a damn thing. What's "truth" anyway? The truth is we need myths. If we had to face the truth in our lives, we'd all be jumpin' off a bridge.

JOE: Guess'n it keeps people from killin' themselves and makes me'n Katie rich, then it's okay by me.

(RING exits as FANS enter. JOE crosses to the entering KATIE who is pasting clippings into a scrapbook.)

FAN 1: Katie Jackson is baseball mad!

FAN 2: Has the fever and has it bad!   26

FAN 1: Katie Jackson sees all the games.

FAN 2: Knows the players by their first names.

BOTH: Katie Jackson is baseball mad!

(The FANS exit.)

KATIE: Listen to this, Joey. "Like Gilgamesh when he built the walls of Uruk, Shoeless Joe showed superhuman strength as he clobbered the Chisox for Cleveland's fourth straight win."

JOE: Gil Gamesh? What team does he play for?

KATIE: He's not a ballplayer, honey, he's the hero of an epic poem.

JOE: Epic what?

KATIE: Poem. I got this book outta the library.

(She reads.)   27

KATIE: "You are the fire that goes out,

You are the pitch…"

JOE: He's a pitcher! Now I remember 'im! Hit against 'im in Philly. He could really fire the ball.

KATIE: It's a different kinda pitch.

(She reads.)

"You are the pitch that sticks to the hand."

JOE: Hit me with his first pitch! Damn near broke my hand!

KATIE: No, honey. Just listen.

(She reads.)

"You are the pitch that sticks to the hand

of the one who carries the bucket."

JOE: Yeah, I did step in the bucket once or twice when I was with the A's.

KATIE: Joe, be serious. Gilgamesh wasn't a baseball player, pitcher or otherwise. This here poem was written 4,000 years ago. Long before baseball was even invented.

JOE: Then why's Ring writin' 'bout him 'steada me?

KATIE: Silly, he's sayin' y'er a hero like the great Gilgamesh.

JOE: So, it's jus' Ring and his damn myth makin'. Don't make no sense to me.

KATIE: Don't have to make no sense, s'long's it makes us money.

JOE: Guess y'er right. If it makes us rich, Ring can make up all the myths he wants.

(BLACKOUT. LIGHTS UP

on JOE warming up as he

overhears two VETS.) 29

VET 1: He collects hairpins. And his wife keeps a scrapbook.

VET 2: It's his talkin' to his bat what gets me.

VET 1: Talks to his stupid bat. Crazy. Crazy as a loon.

(The VETS exit laughing

as RING enters.)

JOE: Don't ya pay them no mind, Betsy, those bums callin' ya names…makes ya mad, don't it? That's good. Take it out on the ball. That's what I do. Somebody makes me mad, I make like I see their ugly face on the ball. Then I wanna hit it even harder. Smash that bastard. Drive his nose all the way into his brain.

(JOE swings Betsy.)

RING: That's quite a piece of lumber you got there, Jackson.

JOE: Her name's Betsy…Black Betsy. She's more'n jus' a piece of lumber.

RING: Right…Black Betsy…I'm sorry.

JOE: It's okay. Betsy forgives ya.

RING: Forgives me? She tell you that?

JOE: She tells me whatever's on her mind. How she's feelin'. Whether she's up to facin' Walter Johnson's fastball today.

RING: What if she's not up to snuff?

JOE: I jus' coax her a littl'. Tell her how much I need her. How I wouldn't be up here if it weren't fer her. Y'know, those kinda things.

RING: Can I hold her?

JOE: I don't know…don't let…   31

RING: …I'll be gentle…I promise.

JOE: Guess it'd be OK. Be careful. She ain't used to nobody, but me.

(JOE gives the bat to RING

RING: Whoa, she's heavy. What's she weigh?

JOE: She don't like me tellin' her weight t nobody…Y'know how a female can be.

VOICE: Now batting for Cleveland…Shoeless Jo Jackson!

JOE: 'Scuse me. Let's go git 'em, Betsy!

RING: (*Writes in notebook.*) Talks to his bat! This guy' a gold mine.

(JOE swings Betsy as KATIE enters.

KATIE: That makes 233 hits ya got this season! I've been a countin' ev'ry one.

JOE: Jus' keep givin' me them hairpins, honey. I'm startin' to like some of this myth makin'.

KATIE: So'm I if it makes us rich.

JOE: Can't read or write, but nobody livin' or dead's ever hit a ball harder.

KATIE: Let me teach ya how to write yer name, Joe.

JOE: Why would I wanna do that?

KATIE: Y'er a big star now, honey. Ya wanna sign yer name fer all the little boys wantin' yer autergraph, don't ya?

RING: A record 233 hits in his first full season! Joe was ready to become a part of the mythology, to be one of the anointed. A Big-League Baseball Idol.

(BLACKOUT. LIGHTS UP.)

(An UMPIRE PRIEST and ALTAR BOY enter.)

PRIEST: (*Chants.*) It's a game of inches,

Where he had a notion,

To score in spurts,

As he knocked the cover

Off the baa-aall.

ALTAR BOY: Knocked the cover off the baa-aall.

PRIEST: He brushed him back,

With a purpose pitch,

With the bases loaded,

To protect his hitters,

And oh, those bases on baa-aalls.

ALTAR BOY: Oh, those bases on baa-aalls.

PRIEST: He came to play,

During the June swoon,

Hitting a lazy fly ball,

Off the handle,

Holy coo-ooww.

ALTAR BOY: Holy coo-ooww.

PRIEST: (*Crosses himself.*)   Bovinus   Sanctus...
Baseball is more than a game to me, it's a religion. Our
National Pastime and it's impossible to understand
America without understanding baseball.

(*RING enters.*)

RING: "Impossible to understand America without
understanding baseball." I like that!

PRIEST: And now I summon thee, Shoeless Joe, to take
thy rightful place, as thou art one of the chosen.

(JOE enters and crosses to the PRIEST.)

PRIEST: Your face shall be seen on holy pictures to be cherished by children everywhere. You're Shoeless Joe, an American Hero.

> *(The PRIEST takes a baseball*
>
> *card from his pocket and gives*
>
> *it to the beaming ALTAR BOY.)*

Your card will be worth three Napoleon Lajoie's or two Smokey Joe Wood's.

RING: Charles Dickens once said that Americans no sooner set up an idol firmly than they are sure to pull it down and dash it into fragments. Any man who attains a high place among Americans may date his downfall from that moment.

(The PRIEST anoints JOE'S forehead.)

PRIEST: Join the ranks of the elite…Honus Wagner, Cy Young, Christy Mathewson and the immortal Ty Cobb.

(TY COBB enters as the PRIEST and JOE exit.) 36

RING: The immortal Ty Cobb!

COBB: Whaddya want?

RING: Is it true that it's not whether you win or lose, but how you play the game?

COBB: Bullshit!

RING: Is it true what they say about you?

COBB: What's that!?

RING: That you're "possessed by the Furies."

COBB: "Possessed by the Furies," my ass. As I always say, "It helps if you help 'em beat themselves." I never woulda survived without that philosophy. Hell, I'm even more successful in the business world than I am in baseball if that's possible. I made millions as one of the original investors in Coca Cola.

RING: And you can't understand America withou understanding Coca Cola.

(RING exits as the BOY

shyly crosses to COBB.

BOY: Mr. Cobb, I want to be a great hitter just like you

(The BOY swings a bat awkwardly

COBB: No, son, that ain't the way! If ya wanna be great hitter like Ty Cobb, ya gotta be real scientific abou it.

BOY: Scientific? Y'mean like biology or somethin'?

COBB: Naw, not like book learnin'. Ya gotta thin when you're up there. Ya gotta try'n outsmart ye opponent, hittin' the ball where ya want it to go.

BOY: Then I'll be a great hitter like you and Shoeles Joe?

3

COBB: Son, Shoeless Joe's an entirely different kinda hitter. He's what ya'd call a natural hitter.

BOY: Natural? Is that better'n you?

COBB: No!!!...I mean, no, son. Joe don't think when he hits. He just swings'n hopes for the best. He's the greatest natural hitter in the history of the game...But I think my way's better. I remember the 1911 season, Joe's first full year in the Majors. He was leading me by nine points...or was it nineteen? Anyway, he had a big lead over me with only six games to go.

BOY: Wow! What happened?

COBB: Well, just hold still'n I'll tell ya. As fate would have it, Joe'n me were playin' each other in those final games. We felt a special sorta kinship, us both bein' from the South. Whenever I'd see Joe, he'd always greet me the same way.

(JOE enters and waves at TY.)

JOE: Hi, Ty, what's new?

COBB: Get lost! Yessiree, I'd give 'im the cold shoulder whenever we passed on the field.

JOE: Is somethin' the matter, Ty?

COBB: Joe was so hurt by my behavior that he couldn't concentrate on his game. Like most ballplayers, when ya stop concentratin' ya stop hittin'. I can still see poor ol' Joe goin' up to the plate.

> *(JOE, with his shoulders slumped,*
>
> *goes up to hit. He drags his bat*
>
> *and looks sad-eyed at COBB.)*

First pitch was down around Joe's ankles.

> *(JOE swings high.)*

Next pitch was high but Joe swung low.

> *(JOE swings low.)*

Joe was 'bout ready to give up. Missed the last pitch by a mile and fell right on his ass…I mean, his be-hind.

> *(JOE swings listlessly and falls.)*

COBB: Joe hit .408 that year. But before ya know it, I passed 'im for the battin' title. Hittin' .408 and finishin' second! That's how I used science...my gift for psychology to beat Shoeless Joe Jackson out of the batting title.

BOY: Thanks, Mr. Cobb, you're the greatest!

(The BOY shakes COBB'S hand and exits.)

COBB: Like I always say, it helps if ya help 'em beat themselves.

(JOE stands and confronts COBB.)

JOE: That's horseshit! I's never ahead of you in hittin' one day that whole season. That never happened and ya know it, Ty. You know it ain't so!

COBB: It ain't?

JOE: No, it ain't!

41

COBB: Yeah…But don't it make great folklore!

(*BLACKOUT*)

VOICE: JACKSON!!

> (*LIGHTS UP on the office of
> CHARLES COMISKEY, the
> owner of the Chicago White
> Sox. He is a prosperous,
> somewhat overweight man.
> He is standing by his desk
> with team secretary,
> HARRY GREY.*)

COMISKEY: That's who we need to pull this team together! Harry, I want you to catch the next train to Cleveland and get me Shoeless Joe.

GREY: Mr. Comiskey, they're going to want an awful lot for him.

COMISKEY: Cleveland's on the verge of bankruptcy. Here's a blank check. Find out how much they want and fill in the figure yourself.

(COMISKEY signs the check and hands it to GREY who exits as 2 REPORTERS enter.)

REPORTER 1: How's the Old Roman? Got any news for us today?

COMISKEY: *(Pours champagne.)* Drink up, boys. Everything's on me. I think I'm going to have a big surprise for you in the near future and I see no harm in our celebrating a little early.

REPORTER 2: What's the surprise, Mr. Comiskey?

REPORTER 1: Yeah, Commy, what's up?

COMISKEY: Well, boys, it may be a little early to giv
you the big news, but I think I made a deal today that wi
turn this ball club completely around. If things work ou
as I've planned, Shoeless Joe Jackson will be wearing
White Sox uniform in the very near future.

REPORTER 2: Shoeless Joe!

REPORTER 1: How'd you ever convince Cleveland t
let him go?

COMISKEY: I let my money do the convincing for me
Cleveland's had some bad luck moneywise lately. A
you know, I'm doing quite well financially myself. S
I figure they'll help me…if I help them.

REPORTER 2: Jackson may be just what you need t
win a pennant.

REPORTER 1: The pennant, hell, with Shoeless Joe an
your pitching staff, you're bound to win a World Serie

COMISKEY: That's right. I don't think my pitchers will be able to complain about a lack of hitting support after we get Joe Jackson...I feel humble at a time like this, fellas...

(*REPORTERS mumble in fun disgust.*)
Humble and reflective. Who would've thought when I was just another ballplayer 25 years ago that I'd one day be the sole owner of a Major League ball club?

REPORTER 2: Just shows ya what good clean livin' can accomplish.

(COMISKEY laughs and takes a
drink of champagne directly
from the bottle. BLACKOUT.
LIGHTS UP on JOE and KATIE
who walk along a Cleveland
street.)

KATIE: What a wonderful show!

JOE: It was ok...Which character was Hamlet?

45

KATIE: D'ya mean to say that ya watched the whole show without knowin'…

JOE: Just foolin', darlin'. But if ya ask me, he shoulda bumped off his uncle in the first scene. Then we coulda gone home early.

KATIE: I thought you enjoyed it. Durin' intermission ya…

JOE: Yeah, I liked it. Coulda used some singin' and dancin', though.

(KATIE playfully punches JOE'S

arm as a NEWSBOY enters.)

KATIE: We could never see a show like that back home in Brandon Mill!

NEWSBOY: EXTRA! EXTRA! READ ALL ABOUT IT! "COMISKEY CONS CLEVELAND! SHOELESS SHIPPED TO CHI!"

JOE: What the?!!

(*JOE grabs a paper and hands it to KATIE.*)

KATIE: *(Reads.)* "Charles Comiskey, owner of the Chicago White Sox, purchased the contract of baseball star Shoeless Joe Jackson for 65,000 dollars today…"

JOE: I ain't goin'!

KATIE: Wait a minute, Joey!

JOE: It'll be the same in Chicago like it was in Philly! People ridin' me all the time.

KATIE: If he paid all that money for ya, he must want ya awful bad.

JOE: I don't care how much he wants me, he ain't gonna get me. Maybe I'll jus' show 'em all and jump to the Federal League!

KATIE: You can't do that. That league probably won't last long. Give 'im a chance, Joe.

(JOE pays the NEWSBOY who now recognizes him.)

JOE: Well, guess I could...

KATIE: Could what?

JOE: Give 'im one chance.

NEWSBOY: Mr. Jackson! Can I have your autograph? You're my favoritest player!

KATIE: Go ahead, Joey. Do it like I showed ya.

(JOE slowly signs a newspaper.)

NEWSBOY: Bet I can get six bits for this!

(The NEWSBOY grabs the
newspaper and exits running.
BLACKOUT. LIGHTS UP on
COMISKEY sitting at his desk
as HARRY GREY enters.)

GREY: Excuse me, Mr. Comiskey, but Chick Gandil is
waiting to see you.

(GREY exits and White Sox
first baseman, CHICK
GANDIL enters.)

COMISKEY: Chick, what can I do for you today?

CHICK: You wanted to talk to me about my contract for
next season.

COMISKEY: Of course.

(COMISKEY opens a drawer and

pulls out a contract. He hands i

to CHICK.)

CHICK: There must be some mistake, Mr. Comiskey.

COMISKEY: Mistake?

CHICK: Y'er offerin' me 4,000 dollars. That's wha
I'm makin' this year.

COMISKEY: I'm quite aware of what you're earnin
this year, Mr. Gandil. As I'm sure you know, we kee
excellent records. There's no mistake.

CHICK: But I'm havin' one of my best seasons. I wa
hopin' ya might consider givin' me a raise.

COMISKEY: Oh, I thought about it. But after ver
serious consideration, I decided against offering you
raise.

CHICK: Mr. Comiskey, sir, I feel I been makin' steady improvement at my position.

COMISKEY: That depends on how you define "improvement."

CHICK: I got a pretty good idea what the word means.

COMISKEY: Perhaps my standards are too high. My wife is always insisting they are. I presume you know how women are.

CHICK: Yeah, I've known one or two in my…

COMISKEY: …But I've always felt that the reason I have accomplished as much as I have in life is because of my high standards, Chuck.

CHICK: Chick.

COMISKEY: Come again?

CHICK: Chick. The name's Chick, not Chuck.

COMISKEY: Of course…Chick. The problem with most ballplayers is they don't plan for the future. When I played, I not only worked on my baseball, but also my life strategy.

CHICK: Mr. Comiskey, this is all very intrestin', but…

COMISKEY: …You're a very good player, Mr. Gandil.

CHICK: Uh…Thank you, sir…and…uh…that's why I think I'm entitled…

COMISKEY: But you are not without…your flaws. That game in Detroit. The most important series of the year. How many times did you strike out?

CHICK: It was four…four times…I was hopin' you'd forgot.

COMISKEY: I never forget. That's what made me so fine a ballplayer. I remembered everything about the opposing players: Their strengths; their weaknesses. How to get them rattled...

CHICK: I ain't rattled!

COMISKEY: Of course, you're not...We'll be very sorry to lose you if you decide not to sign, Mr. Gandil. But let me remind you that you really have no place to go, unless you consider returning to your former occupation in the coal mines an attractive alternative. You wouldn't make more than 4,000 dollars a year working in the mines and I don't think that the hours would be nearly as good. As far as your baseball career is concerned, Mr. Gandil, you belong to me. As you know, the reserve clause makes you my property.

CHICK: What about the 10-Day clause?

COMISKEY: What about it?

CHICK: I'll sign if ya scratch it out.

COMISKEY: How could you expect me, as a responsible businessman, to do such a thing? Really, Mr. Gandil, if you're injured, should I be expected to continue to pay you more than 10 days after the date of your injury? No business in America could survive if it operated like that. Life's a gamble, Mr. Gandil. I'm gambling that you'll continue to help me while you're gambling that you won't get hurt. And I think that there's more chance of your getting hurt in the mines than on the ball field. Don't you agree…Chuck?

(He hands CHICK a pen. He reluctantly signs.)

(BLACKOUT. LIGHTS UP

on REPORTERS and RING

sitting at a bar.)

REPORTER 1: Did you hear about Hoot Evans?

RING: No. What happened?

REPORTER 1: He slipped in the shower. Broke his tailbone.

RING: Broke the old coccyx, huh? Ouch.

REPORTER 1: I'm serious, and with the 10-Day clause, he's not gonna get paid anymore. Hoot's out the whole season. So, some of us guys, we're takin' up a collection for him. I know he plays for Detroit…

RING: …Y'er not getting my beer money.

REPORTER 1: He's a ballplayer. He's gotta make a buck, too. What would you do if you broke your arm'n couldn't write anymore?

RING: I'd write with my toes.

REPORTER 2: Use my nose.

REPORTER 1: You guys are heartless.

RING: Okay, okay. Whaddya want? Will a buck make you happy?

REPORTER 1:   From you a nickel would make m
happy.

RING: From the bottom of my heart.

>   *(RING gives a dollar to*

>   *REPORTER 1 and turr*

>   *to REPORTER 2.)*

Come on, match it, Ted!

REPORTER 2: Gee, I don't know. Promised the wife.

RING: Don't strain yourself.

REPORTER 2: Here, Gus. Here's two dollars!

RING: Aw, c'mon now!

REPORTER 1:   Well, now it's gettin' real intrestin
Gonna up that, Ring?

RING: Here's five. Now go away.

REPORTER 1: Gonna match that, Ted? Huh, Ted?

(RING and GUS laugh as TED matches.)
(BLACKOUT. LIGHTS UP on COMISKEY waving to the cheering crowd from his box as RING and 2 REPORTERS enter.)

VOICE: The CHI-CA-GOOOO WHITE SOX!!!

COMISKEY: And in the progressive tradition of the White Sox ball club, I proclaim today to be the first "Ladies' Day" in baseball history. All ladies, accompanied by a gentleman, will be admitted free!

RING: You ought to run for mayor, Commy.

COMISKEY: *(Waves to cheering crowd.)* Ring, I'd rather win a pennant than an election...And now, Ladies and Gentlemen, it is with great pleasure that I introduce

COMISKEY: *(cont.)* the newest addition to our White Sox family, and we are one big happy family here in Chicago, aren't we?

(The crowd cheers.)

And here he is. The greatest natural hitter in the history of the game, Shoeless Joe Jackson!

(JOE enters waving to the cheering crowd. The BAT BOY enters and hands him Black Betsy. JOE crosses to COMISKEY'S box, saluting him by extending his right arm as he holds Black Betsy like a sword. COMISKEY laughs and responds with a "thumbs up." COMISKEY pours champagne for REPORTERS as KATIE enters.)

KATIE: Here's another hairpin for ya, Joey.

JOE: That'll be my welcome-to-Chicago hairpin.

KATIE: Will ya look at that stadium!

JOE: Ain't it somethin'? They say Mr. Comiskey paid for it right outta his own pocket.

KATIE: The papers say he paid 65,000 dollars for ya. He must be the richest man in Chicago if he can throw money around like that.

JOE: They say he's tryin' to put together the best team money can buy so he can bring a World Series to Chicago. We get in the Series, it'll mean more money for us.

KATIE: Maybe all these hairpins I been givin' ya are bringin' good luck after all.

> *(KATIE exits.)*
>
> *(Gambler, SLEEPY BILLY, holding*
>
> *his ticket, and two FANS enter.*
>
> *BILLY crosses to RING, who is*
>
> *sitting and reading a newspaper.)*

FAN 1: Sleepy Billy's a gamblin' man.

FAN 2: One of the reckless kind.

FAN 1: A gamer sport in all the world.

FAN 2: I'm sure you couldn't find.

RING: (*Points.*) General Admission's that way.

> *(BILLY shows him his ticket.*
> *as the FANS exit.)*

SLEEPY BILLY: You're in my seat.

> *(RING reluctantly moves over one seat.)*

RING: It's all yours.

SLEEPY BILLY: I never could figure ya out, Ring Lard-butt.

RING: Figure what out?

SLEEPY BILLY: How a smart guy like you could spend so much time at a ballpark.

RING: I get paid for it. I'm a baseball writer.

SLEEPY BILLY: Yeah, I know, but I have the feelin' you'd be here even if ya weren't gettin' paid. Am I right?

RING: Guess you could call me a "professional fan."

SLEEPY BILLY: Now, me, I come for one reason and one reason only.

RING: You like Comiskey Park franks, am I right?

SLEEPY BILLY: No, I haven't had one in years, and ya know somethin'? I can still taste it.

RING: Same thing happens to me.   61

SLEEPY BILLY: So, we do have somethin' in commo
after all.

RING: Yeah, maybe so 'cause being around guys lik
you leaves a very bad taste in my mouth every time.

SLEEPY BILLY: I don't know why ya don't like me.

RING: I could think of about two dozen reasons.

SLEEPY BILLY: Such as?

RING: What about you and Hal Chase?

SLEEPY BILLY: Prince Hal's a pal o' mine. So wha

RING: I hear he's a real pal.

SLEEPY BILLY: Whaddya mean?

RING: I hear you two are partners. That he throw
games for you all the time.   6

SLEEPY BILLY: A gross exaggeration, my friend. He may boot one for me now and then…as a personal favor. I make it worth his while. So what?

RING: I'm just old fashioned. Always felt the grand old game should be kept pure. Like when I was a kid.

SLEEPY BILLY: Sure, it's a kids' game. But when there's money to be made, men are gonna want to make it. Stick with me. I could make us both rich.

RING: No, thanks.

SLEEPY BILLY: What's the matter? Don't ya like money? That's unAmerican.

RING: Sure, I like money. Just not that kind of money.

ANNOUNCER: Ladies and Gentlemen! The winner of the pregame throwing contest with a toss of 396 feet, Shoeless Joe Jackson!

(The crowd cheers as RING crosses to JOE.)   63

RING: That was some throw, Jackson. Your place in baseball mythology is secure.

JOE: Must be gettin' old. I can usually make 400 feet without hardly tryin'…What's all this nonsense you been writin'?

RING: Which nonsense is that, Joe?

JOE: Somethin' 'bout me goin' to a restaurant'n drinkin' from some finger bowl. What the hell's a finger bowl anyway?

RING: If you don't know, then maybe you have drunk from one.

JOE: Why'd ya write that? Makin' me out to be some kinda hillbilly.

RING: I wasn't writing about you, Joe Jackson, the man. I was writing about "Shoeless Joe," the myth.

JOE: More like Joe Jackson, the fool. 64

RING: It humanizes a baseball god. The fans love it.

JOE: Maybe the fans love yer humanizin' me, but I sure don't.

RING: Don't worry, Joe, you'll thank me in the long run.

(RING exits as JOE'S teammate LEFTY WILLIAMS, enters and crosses to JOE.)

LEFTY: *(Reads article.)* "Shoeless Joe studied the menu pretending to be able to read. After his longtime pal and short-time teammate, Lefty Williams, that's me, ordered ham'n eggs, Joe put down the menu, smiled at the waitress and said, 'That'll be ditto for me'."

JOE: I never said "ditto" in my life! Wonder if I can sue 'em.

LEFTY: Don't worry about it, Joe. This stuff'll make ya popular with the fans. They'll be cheerin' ya from the rafters.

(SLEEPY BILLY greets the entering CHICK.)

SLEEPY BILLY: Chick, my friend! The club's lookin' real good now that ya got Shoeless shit-for-brains on your team.

CHICK: Yeah, he may be dumb, but he just might help us win a World Series or two. I could use the extra dough.

SLEEPY BILLY: Aren't ya tired of playin' for peanuts?

CHICK: Yeah, but it beats the coal mines.

SLEEPY BILLY: Maybe so, maybe so. Look at this crowd. Must be fifty thousand people here. Comiskey must be rakin' it in. What's he payin' ya? Three, four thousand?

CHICK: He's got me by the balls. Look at these suckers. I feel sorry for 'em.

SLEEPY BILLY: Why?

CHICK: Don't they got nuttin' better to do with their time than watch a baseball game? Ya couldn't pay me enough to sit on my butt for three hours watchin' a ball game.

SLEEPY BILLY: There's money to be made, my friend.

CHICK: I'll give ya a tip. Ya see Faber's pitchin' today?

SLEEPY BILLY: Yeah, I figure he can't lose.

CHICK: Red told me his shoulder ain't feelin' so good. And he just got over a touch'a the flu.

SLEEPY BILLY: Intrestin'. Thanks for the tip, Chick. If it pays off, I'll remember ya.   67

CHICK: I was hopin' you'd say that.

(*White Sox coach KID GLEASON enters*

KID: What's goin' on here?

CHICK: Nuttin's goin' on, Kid. Ain't a guy got a rigl to talk to his friends? Mr. Comiskey would be glad to see us fraternizin' with the fans.

KID: How ya figure that?

CHICK: It's good for the public relations.

(*CHICK crosses to the enterin White Sox shortstop, SWEDE RISBERG, as KID confronts BILLY.*)

KID: Why don't you get outta here?!

SLEEPY BILLY: I paid my admission, Kid.

KID: Stay away from my players. I heard what ya offered some of them Cubbies.

SLEEPY BILLY: I offered my support, Kid. My moral support.

KID: Your kinda "moral" support we can do without.

(KID exits as SWEDE and CHICK cross to JOE as the crowd cheers.)

SWEDE: You better enjoy those cheers, Jackson.

CHICK: Swede's right, Joe. They don't pay yer mortgage, but I guess they do make ya feel good.

SWEDE: Look at FFC up there, passin' 'round that expensive champagne like it's water.

(COMISKEY and the REPORTERS

roar with laughter.)

JOE: FFC?

CHICK: Fat-Fucking-Commy. He sure is a generous soul...Why do you play for him, Swede?

SWEDE: Same reason as you, Chick, to make me some money.

CHICK: But we ain't gettin' paid what we're worth, are we, Swede?

SWEDE: We sure as shit ain't, Chick.

CHICK: Why's that, Swede?

SWEDE: 'Cause we're Mr. Comiskey's property, Chick.

CHICK: And he don't never let us forget it, do he?

SWEDE: He sure as shit don't.

CHICK: Don't expect him to be too generous with ya, Joe. I don't care what yer lifetime battin' average is.

(An UMPIRE enters.)

UMPIRE: Play Ball!

ANNOUNCER: Batting for the White Sox...Swee-eeede Risberg!

(SWEDE goes up to the plate, while
JOE and LEFTY sit on a bench as
CHICK waits on deck.)

LEFTY: It's true, Commy's a cheap son of a bitch, Joe.

UMPIRE: Stee-eerike one!   71

LEFTY: Ya just gotta figure out other ways to make the big dough.

JOE: Like how?

UMPIRE: Stee-eerike two!

LEFTY: Vaudeville.

UMPIRE: Stee-eerike three, y'er out!

> (*SWEDE throws his bat to CHICK, turns and punches out the UMP.*)

> (*BLACKOUT. LIGHTS UP on JOE and LEFTY sitting on a bench in the White Sox locker room.*)

JOE: Vaudeville? Why would anyone pay to see me in some vaudeville show?

LEFTY: Y'er a hero, a legend. Ya ain't gonna get rich playin' for FFC.

JOE: I don't wanna be one of them ballplayers gives his all to the game'n winds up havin' nuttin' to show fer it. Don't seem fair, but vaudeville?

LEFTY: I gave up long ago 'spectin' life to be fair. Mathewson and Cobb done it. All ya gotta do is make some half-assed speech about yer baseball career'n they'll pay ya big money! It's all just waitin' for somebody like you in vaudeville.

(LEFTY exits as the voice

of an EMCEE is heard.)

EMCEE: And now Ladies and Gentlemen, the beautiful Temple Theatre is proud to present the greatest natural hitter in the history of baseball, Shoeless Joe Jackson!

JOE: Evenin', Ladies and Gentlemen. Thank you for coming to see my show tonight. Throughout my baseball career I've been asked, "Joe, how did ya ever get that nickname of yours...Shoeless Joe, that is? 'Well,' I always reply, 'It's a long story, but if ya got the time, I'll be happy to tell ya how I acquired my nickname...Shoeless Joe, that is'." Mama and Daddy

JOE: *(cont.)* didn't name me Shoeless, although they te
me they considered it since I was born withou
shoes…on my feet, that is. Ya see, I had just gotten m
some new spiked shoes that raised some terrible blister
I decided I'd play without shoes on and, as I was runnir
'round the bases in the process of hittin' a home run,
fella in the stands shouted, "Oh, ya shoeless son of a…
Oops, I mean ya shoeless so-and-so. Thought it wa
kinda silly at first, but now I don't mind. In fact, if I'
lucky enough to have a son someday, maybe I'll ju
name him Shoeless Joe Jr. Or, if I have a daughte
Shoeless Josephine.

HECKLER 1: Get off the stage, you illiterate linthead

HECKLER 2: I want my money back!

(KATIE enters and crosses to JOE

JOE: How'd I do?

KATIE: I think ya'd best forget about a career in th
the-a-ter, Joe.

JOE: Was I that bad?

KATIE: Worse.

JOE: Maybe my act would work out better down South where they respect me. These Northern folk, all they can do is criticize me and talk 'bout how dumb they think I am. I was hopin' if they heard me tell my story they might change their...

KATIE: Ya gotta learn to read, Joey, then maybe they'll change their opinion of ya. And ya can prepare yerself for a career outside baseball. First thing is ya have to memorize the alphabet. Ya almost had it learned last week...A...B...

JOE: I'm too old to learn. Maybe that heckler was right. What did he call me? An illiterate linthead? Maybe that ain't so bad.

KATIE: Why would ya think that?

JOE: It's part of my myth. Can't read or write, but it don't matter. All that matters is the way I play baseball. That's the only way I can earn me some respect.

KATIE: They won't respect ya all that much if yer battin' average goes down. D'ya want these Yankees thinkin' y'er ignorant yer whole life? And what if ya get injured and can't play no more? If ya break yer leg on openin' day ya'd only get paid fer 10 days. Ya'd have to go back to the mills. Yer myth won't matter much then.

JOE: I ain't never goin' back there no matter what happens.

KATIE: Ya may have no choice. You players are the ones the fans pay to see but, it's the owners like Comiskey who're gettin' rich. Jus' like back home. The bosses get rich…

JOE: …While the workers stay poor.

KATIE: Seems like the whole game in every field is fixed in favor of the bosses. 76

JOE: I know it's unfair. If there was some way I could get back at Comiskey, I'd do it fer sure. We gotta figure out how.

KATIE: We know how. Ya gotta show Comiskey ya can make a good livin' outside of baseball. He'll think he'll have to pay ya more to keep ya. That's why he don't pay ya and the other players what he should. He knows there's nothin' else y'all can do.

JOE: I heard he's payin' Eddie Collins 15,000 dollars a year! That's more'n double what I make. Collins is a good player, but nobody can say he's better'n me.

KATIE: He pays Collins that much because he's got a college degree. He knows Eddie could do very well even if he quit baseball tomorrow. That's what we've gotta do.

JOE: What?

KATIE: Show Comiskey that he needs us more'n we need him. When we set up our business...

JOE: …What kinda business, Katie?

KATIE: Dry cleanin', Joe, dry cleanin'.

JOE: Dry cleanin'?

KATIE: Ya! I was readin' 'bout it in a magazine. They
say it's the "wave of the future."

JOE: "Wave of the future"? I'd rather own me a liquor
store.

> (*LEFTY runs onstage as patriotic*
>
> *martial music is heard.*)

LEFTY: Let's get goin', Joe! We gotta practice our
marchin' drill!

JOE: Our what?

LEFTY: Our marchin' drill! What with the war on in Europe, Commy wants us to be prepared. Says we'll be fined if we don't do it right.

(*FANS enter as KATIE exits.*)

FAN 1: America, I raised a boy for you.

FAN 2: America, you'll find him staunch and true.

FAN 1: Place a gun upon his shoulder.

FAN 2: He's ready to die or do.

(*SWEDE and CHICK enter as the FANS exit. The players march holding their bats to their shoulders like rifles. KID GLEASON enters.*)

KID: Left…Left…Left…   79

PLAYERS: Here's to the Kaiser,

The Limburger cheese.

May the swell in his head,

Go down to his knees.

May he break his damn neck,

On the Hindenburg line.

JOE: And go to hell croakin',

"The Watch on the Rhine."

(RING enters.)

RING: World War 1, "the war to end all wars." Th
Americans helped defeat the evil Huns and the futur
was looking good. To many, baseball seemed t
symbolize all that was good about society. In 191
Comiskey told his players that he'd give them a bonus
they won the World Series. They did win, beating th
Giants in six.

(The players celebrate their win

RING: Commy's "bonus" was a case of champagne that tasted like stale piss.

> *(The players taste the champagne.*
>
> *They gag and spit and cough.)*

 By 1919, they were ready to revolt.

> *(RING exits.)*

CHICK: We've had it, Kid.

SWEDE: Either ya tell Comiskey to pay us what we're worth or we walk.

KID: Whaddya mean?

LEFTY: We'll strike if we don't get what we want.

KID: Are y'all crazy? If ya do somethin' stupid, that bastard will kick your asses outta the game so...

SWEDE: How's he gonna win another World Series if he does that? 81

LEFTY: The way we figure, he's got no choice.

CHICK: He'll have to pay us when ya tell him we're standin' together on this.

KID: Will you guys promise not to strike or do nuttin' drastic if I don't get results?

                    (The players don't respond.)

All I can do is give it a try. But I'm not promisin' ya nuttin'!

                    (BLACKOUT. LIGHTS UP on

                    COMISKEY'S office. RING

                    writes as COMISKEY dictates.)

COMISKEY: To me, baseball is as honorable as any other business. If it weren't, it wouldn't be able to survive as the greatest pastime in the world. Crookedness and baseball do not mix. This year, 1919, is the greatest season of them all and I think the White Sox are the greatest bunch I ever saw on a ball field. I am eager for the battles to begin and all the boys are confident.   82

RING: Thanks a lot, Commy.

(RING exits as KID enters.)

COMISKEY: Yes, what is it, Kid?

KID: I hate to bother ya, sir, but I promised the boys I'd talk to ya. Y'know, I agree with what ya was sayin' 'bout them. Hell, they're the best bunch of players I've ever seen, too. It's a thrill watchin' Buck Weaver now, ain't it? Cobb says he's the best third baseman he's ever seen. Imagine that! He was makin' an error a day when he first come up. I musta hit him a million grounders, practicin' with him. And Hap Felsch....

COMISKEY: ...What's the point, Kid?

KID: Well, sir, since business' been so much better'n last season, they was wonderin' if ya'd be willin' to renegotiate some of their contracts.

COMISKEY: No. They're grown men. They knew what they were doing when they signed their contracts Nobody put a gun to their heads and forced them to sign

KID: I know that, but ya gotta do somethin'. Some o: 'em have been talkin' about organizin' some kinda strike or somethin'.

COMISKEY: You tell them if any player of mine gets involved in any kind of strike "or somethin'," I'll see to it that they'll be driven from organized baseball forever

KID: Are ya gonna send me back empty-handed? Whatta I tell 'em?

COMISKEY: Tell them that if they win the pennant, I'l give them a bonus.

> (*COMISKEY exits. KID crosses to
> the entering players. KID shrugs
> and makes a gesture as if to say
> "What more can I do?" The players
> react angrily as they exit. RING
> enters.)* 84

RING: How you doing, Kid?

KID: Not so great.

RING: I'm surprised.

KID: Whaddya mean?

RING: I'd think you'd be happy. You've achieved your goal.

KID: What's that?

RING: You're headed to another World Series. You are the manager of the best team in baseball. Some say the best team ever.

KID: Yeah, well, let me tell ya somethin', it ain't no bed o' roses.

RING: Why?

KID: (*Starts to exit.*) Never mind.

RING: Are the rumors true?

KID: What rumors?

RING: There's been a lotta talk goin' 'round.

KID: What kinda talk?

RING: You know, Kid, the usual kind. Discontente
players…unhappy about the size of their paychecl
…that sort of thing.

KID: I'm sick o' them crybabies! They're lucky the
got the chance to play ball at all. There's plenty o' guy
would give their right nut for a chance to play ball for
livin'. Back in my day, we played for the love o' th
game…These players today…It's not every guy gets
chance to earn good…Earn any kinda money at a
playin' a kids' game.

RING: But, Kid, you sat out last season because of
salary dispute with Commy, didn't you?   8

KID: Yeah, well…We was able to work things out.

RING: Williams and Jackson get paid less than half what stars on other teams are making. Guess they haven't been able to "work things out."

KID: I don't know nuttin' 'bout that…All you writers…Bunch o' know-it-alls…Y'er probably helpin' stir up this "discontent" y'er talkin' about. Who knows what they might do?

RING: What might they do?

KID: Never mind. I got nuttin' to say to ya…and ya can quote me on that!

(KID exits as COMISKEY enters.)

COMISKEY: You upsetting the help again, Ring?

RING: I understand your "help" isn't so happy.

COMISKEY: There's never been a hint of discontent on any ball club of mine. I've always treated my employees like family. You forget I was a player once myself.

RING: Didn't you help organize a league back in '90?

COMISKEY: That's right. My association with what we old-time ballplayers affectionately refer to as "The Brotherhood" is one of the proudest accomplishments of my life. I was willing to stand up for fair wages for ballplayers back in 1890 and I'm willing to stand up now.

RING: You always were a stand-up guy, Commy.

COMISKEY: And I don't want to read about any "discontent." A respectable salary, the love of millions of kids, the envy of adults...What more could any ballplayer want?

RING: (*Watches Comiskey exit.*) Turned out some of the White Sox players wanted more...much more.

(BLACKOUT.)

(LIGHTS UP on CHICK and

SLEEPY BILLY at a bar.)

SLEEPY BILLY: Chick…Chick Gandil.

CHICK: How ya doin', Billy? Long time no see.

SLEEPY BILLY: Yeah, it's been a while. When was it? That time in Boston?

CHICK: Yeah, we tore up that hotel.

SLEEPY BILLY: What happened? I heard they'd never rent to ballplayers again. What was it they called you? A bunch of….

CHICK: …"Unsavory characters." I figured that described us pretty good.

SLEEPY BILLY: I been wantin' to thank ya, Chick. That tip you gave me.   89

CHICK: Which one?

SLEEPY BILLY: Faber. Sore arm. Made a bundle.

CHICK: Don't mention it. Thanks for layin' a few bucks on me...I'm glad I got the chance to talk to ya Billy. I may have somethin' else, 'bout a thousand times bigger'n that Faber tip.

SLEEPY BILLY: Cicotte's shoulder's shot? He won' be pitchin' in the Series?

CHICK: Nah, he's gonna pitch all right. His shoulder's fine. But he ain't gonna win.

SLEEPY BILLY: Whaddya mean? Outside of Roush and Groh the Reds got nobody who can touch him.

CHICK: Do I gotta spell it out for ya, Sleepy? I always thought you was a smart man. If I get Cicotte, I get Williams. If I get Risberg, I get Felsch. If I get...

SLEEPY BILLY: Do you mean?...That's a good one. You're shittin' me, ain't ya? The World Series? Let me buy ya a drink. Wait'll I tell the guys how ya tried to pull my leg. Throw the Series! Ha!

CHICK: It's no joke, Billy. If ya won't pay us, we'll find someone who will. There must be somebody willin' to put up 80 grand to pay eight guys with the guts to throw the Series.

SLEEPY BILLY: Yeah...There must be somebody... Are you serious?

CHICK: My time's too valuable to be playin' games with ya, Billy. It's yer chance to make it to the big time. Whaddya say?

SLEEPY BILLY: I'm in...If ya deliver Jackson.

(BLACKOUT.)

(*LIGHTS UP. A loud bongo drumbeat heard as JOE runs onstage. He stops, looks around and starts to exit SR. Another drumbeat is heard as CHICK enters blocking JOE'S exit. JOE turns and runs SL. Another drumbeat is heard as his exit is blocked by the entering SWEDE who is tossing a ball in the air. SWEDE tries to tag JOE who backs away. SWEDE and CHICK have JOE caught in a rundown. The tempo accelerates and the drumbeats get louder as the scene progresses. SWEDE throws the ball to CHICK.*)

CHICK: You could get 20 grand for a week's work!

(*CHICK tries to tag JOE*

JOE: No!

(CHICK flips the ball to SWEDE.)

SWEDE: Listen to Chick, Joe. Don't be a simp.

(SWEDE starts to tag JOE, who eludes him. SWEDE tosses the ball to CHICK.)

JOE: Get the hell away from me!

CHICK: Listen to Swede, Joe. Don't be stupid. It'll be easy, so easy.

(CHICK advances toward JOE.)

JOE: No! Don't care how easy it'd be.

93

(CHICK flips to SWEDE. They are closing in on JOE.)

SWEDE: C'mon, Joe. I'm tired of playin' for peanuts.

(SWEDE tries to tag JOE who falls.)

JOE: *(Stands.)* Then quit! Y'all can go back to the damn coal mines fer all I care!

(SWEDE throws to CHICK.)

CHICK: One big killin', that's all I need.

(CHICK flips to SWEDE.)

SWEDE: I'm tired of Fat-Fucking-Commy holdin' me by the balls.

(SWEDE flips to CHICK.)

CHICK: C'mon, Joe, 20 grand! Think of it. Twenty grand!

JOE: Twenty grand? I'd get all that dough to....No! I ain't gonna do it!

> *(JOE falls as CHICK and*
> *SWEDE stand over him.)*

CHICK: Play ball, Joe.

JOE: Play ball? That's what I'm wantin' to do.

SWEDE: Play ball with us.

CHICK: You'll be playin' to lose, not win.

SWEDE: It'll be fun...Challengin'.

JOE: Challengin'...How?

CHICK: Makin' it look like we're tryin' to win.

SWEDE: When we're really tryin' to lose.

CHICK: Ya can make more in two weeks than ya made the last three years.

JOE: I wouldn't be his property no more?

CHICK: We wouldn't be Comiskey's slaves no more He loses while we win...

SWEDE: ...by losin'. It'll be fun.

JOE: Fun?

CHICK: Seein' which one of us can make the mos' convincin' loser. Maybe we should give the one who wins a bonus.

SWEDE: And it sure as hell won't be a case of horse piss champagne.

CHICK: Ya can either join us or play ball. We're gonna lose the Series so ya might as well play along.

JOE: I ain't gonna be in it.

CHICK: Y'er in it already so ya might as well stay in it.

JOE: How ya figure that?

CHICK: Y'er in it if ya know about it.

JOE: I can go to the boss and have every damn one of y'all pulled out of the limelight.

CHICK: It wouldn't be well for ya if ya did that.

JOE: Any time ya want me knocked off, then have me knocked off.

CHICK: (*Laughs.*) Ya with us, Joe, or not?

JOE: I'll sleep on it.

CHICK: Sweet dreams…'bout what you'n Katie coul‹
do with all that money…Sleep on it, Joe.

(CHICK and SWEDE exit‹

JOE: Twenty grand. More'n enough fer Katie'n me ‹
set up our own business. Live in comfort. Maybe
should…sleep (*yawns*)…on…it.

(JOE curls up into a ba‹

and sleeps.)

(END OF ACT 1)

(CURTAIN)

<u>ACT 2</u>

SETTING: A Baseball Park.

AT RISE: JOE is in the same position as at
                     the end of ACT 1. RING enters.

RING: The 1919 World Series! The mighty Chicago White Sox against the National League champion Cincinnati Reds. The Sox had been heavily favored, but the odds changed suddenly before the first game. Rumors were rife that something was amiss.

(Two FANS enter as RING exits.)

FAN 1: Lazy Joey, will ya get up?   99

FAN 2: Will ya get up?

FAN 1: Will ya get up?

(KID enters.)

KID: Here's yer glove, Joe. Go out there and shag some flies.

(JOE doesn't move.)

FAN 2: Lazy Joey, will ya get up?

FAN 1: And go out and shag some flies!

(The FANS exit.)

KID: Wake up, Jackson. Get yer ass out there'n shag some flies!

JOE: Don't feel like it.

KID: Whaddya say? I couldn't hear ya.

JOE: I says I don't feel like it. I'm sick. I can't play.

KID: What?

JOE: I'M SICK! I CAN'T PLAY! GOT A SORE ARM!

KID: What the hell ya talkin' about? Ya never had a sore arm in yer life.

JOE: (*Stands.*) Kid, have ya heard anything?

KID: Like what?

JOE: Have ya heard anything 'bout the Series not bein' played...on the square?

KID: Yeah, I heard some rumors.

JOE: Ya have?

KID: I heard the rumors, just like I heard rumors before
last year's Series'n the Series before that'n the Series
before that'n the Series before that. It happens every
year. Gamblers spread rumors to change the odds. Don'
mean nuttin'.

JOE: Bench me, Kid. I got a sore arm. I can hardly lif
it. I can't risk my career just for a World Series, can I?

KID: I'm not gonna bench ya, you should know tha
without askin'. C'mon, Joe, y'er gonna have a grea
Series. Ya probably just got some pregame jitters, that'
all.

>   *(He slaps JOE on the back.)*

Now go out there'n shag some flies.

>   *(JOE exits as KID crosses to*
>
>   *the entering RING, who is*
>
>   *carrying a flask.)*

RING: How's tricks, Kid?

KID: What's up, Ring? Lookin' forward to the game, I see.

RING: *(Drinks from flask.)* You know me, Kid. Nothing like the World Serious.

KID: Yeah, sure.

RING: Just wanted you to know I'll be rooting for you. Maybe I'll put a dollar or two down on you guys.

KID: Maybe that's not such a bright idea.

RING: Why not?

KID: Didn't yer mother tell ya? It ain't nice to bet on baseball games.

(KID exits.)

RING: *(Sings.)* I'm forever blowing ball games,

> Pretty ball games in the air.

> I come from Chi,

> I hardly try....

> *(BLACKOUT. LIGHTS UP on SLEEP*
> *BILLY, who enters and sits down nex*
> *to JOE in the lobby of a Cincinnati*
> *hotel.)*

SLEEPY BILLY: Hey, Joe!

JOE: Hey!...How's everything?

SLEEPY BILLY: Everything's fine...Just fine...Read
to play ball?

JOE: Ready to knock the Reds' blocks off, if that's wh
y'er meanin'.   1(

SLEEPY BILLY: Ready to knock their blocks off?!! What about the plan?

JOE: What plan?

SLEEPY BILLY: You know…the plan. Gandil… Cicotte.

JOE: I don't know nuttin' 'bout what they might be plannin' and prefer not to either.

SLEEPY BILLY: I thought you were in on…Where's Chick?

JOE: Dunno…In on what? I told ya, I ain't in on nuttin'!…This 'bout all them rumors goin' 'round?

> (*BILLY stands and exits quickly. JOE rises and stares after him. BLACKOUT. LIGHTS UP on COMISKEY sitting in a chair in his hotel room. A knocking is heard.*)
> 105

COMISKEY: *(Answers door.)* Joe?! What're you doing here? You should be getting ready for the game.

JOE: *(Enters.)* I don't wanna be in the lineup. I don't wanna be part of no game.

COMISKEY: What're you talking about? You're going to be in the lineup. We can't win without you.

JOE: Please, Mr. Comiskey, I'm beggin' ya.

COMISKEY: Joe, you've got to play. What would we tell the fans…the writers?

JOE: Tell 'em ya suspended me.

COMISKEY: Suspended you? You've never given us any reason to suspend you.

JOE: Tell 'em I was drunk. Tell 'em anything ya want, but leave me outta the Series so there can't be no question.   106

COMISKEY: Question about what?

JOE: 'Bout the rumors.

COMISKEY: Rumors? What rumors?...You're going to play, Joe. We're not going to bench you. We're not going to suspend you. Go on to the ballpark.

JOE: But Mr. Comiskey...

COMISKEY: Go, Joe.

> *(JOE slowly turns and exits. BLACKOUT.*
> *LIGHTS UP on SLEEPY BILLY confronting*
> *CHICK.)*

SLEEPY BILLY: Chick! What the fuck!!

CHICK: What's the matter, Billy?

SLEEPY BILLY: What's the matter? I just got done talkin' to Jackson, that's what's the matter.

CHICK: So?

SLEEPY BILLY: So!? Thought you said he was gonna play ball.

CHICK: Of course he's playin'. He's startin' left field like always.

SLEEPY BILLY: I know he's playin' the game, but is he playin' ball with us?

CHICK: He's playin' along. What makes ya think he's not?

SLEEPY BILLY: Because he told me.

CHICK: What did he tell ya?

SLEEPY BILLY: That he don't know nuttin' abou what's goin' on...the plan. 108

CHICK: He knows. He's just playin' dumb with ya, Billy.

SLEEPY BILLY: He sure don't talk like....

CHICK: Calm down. Trust me. Joe knows what'll happen if he don't play ball...or he should know.

SLEEPY BILLY: Trust you? Guess I got no choice. Game starts in a few hours. Do me a favor.

CHICK: What is it?

SLEEPY BILLY: Give Cicotte a message.

CHICK: Whaddya want me to tell him?

SLEEPY BILLY: Tell him to hit the first batter...if the fix is on.

(CHICK nods and exits. BILLY turns and crosses to the entering RING. SLEEPY pulls out a wad of cash and offers the reporter some money. RING holds up his hand and shakes his head "No". BILLY laughs and crosses to two FANS.)

FAN 1: Isn't this great! Box seats at the World Series

FAN 2: Yeah, I just wish I coulda found me some fo willin' to put some money down on the Reds. I'd willin' to give two-to-one odds.

FAN 1: Look at that!

FAN 2: Cicotte hit the first batter!

FAN 1: He's probably a little nervous. Don't worry.

(SLEEPY BILLY crosses to the FANS.)

SLEEPY BILLY: Pardon me, gentlemen, but did I hear ya say ya'd like to bet some of your hard-earned money on the Sox?

(The FANS look at each other,

stunned by their good fortune.)

FAN 2: We might be willin' to consider it, if the odds're right.

SLEEPY BILLY: How about…even money?

(The FANS can barely conceal their joy.)

FAN 2: Mister, ya got yerself a bet!

(JOE enters carrying Black

Betsy as SLEEPY BILLY and

the FANS exit.)   111

RING: Cicotte got hammered in Game One, allowing five runs in the fourth, including a two-run triple by the opposing pitcher, Dutch Ruether. Joe went hitless in four at-bats but did score the lone White Sox run in the 9-1 debacle.

JOE: *(Talks to his bat.)* What's that, Betsy? Ya hated that game today? Ya never played where the team was tryin' to lose? I hate it, too. Whaddya mean ya think maybe I wasn't doin' my best?! I wasn't tryin' to lose, Betsy, you know me better'n that. Every player has an o-fer plenty of times in his career. I ain't the only one. We jus' gotta try to get through this together...No, I can't talk to Katie. I don't want her to be no part of this.

RING: The whole baseball world was shocked by the Reds' rout, and none more so than the White Sox owner.

(JOE and RING exit as COMISKEY and GREY enter, followed by KID, who is holding a stack of telegrams.)

KID: …And I got another stack in my office.

COMISKEY: What do you think it means, Kid?

KID: I hate to say it, sir, but I didn't like the way some of the boys was playin' today. I know there are always rumors before a Series, but not like this year.

(COMISKEY walks KID to the door.)

COMISKEY: Don't worry, Kid. I think we just had a bad day, that's all.

GREY: After all, we didn't win every game this year.

KID: I know that! But these telegrams…

COMISKEY: …Kid, we'll probably be laughing about this after we clobber Cincinnati tomorrow.

KID: Hope y'er right, sir. It's just…well…I'd use an iron on anybody who'd fuck us over.   113

(*KID exits.*)

COMISKEY: I don't like it, Harry. I never saw Cicotte pitch the way he did today. But what can I do? I can' turn to the illustrious President of the American League Ban Johnson. He hates my guts. He'd use anything to destroy me and my ball club.

GREY: Why don't you get some rest, sir? Like you said to Kid, we'll be laughing about this tomorrow.

COMISKEY: Do you think I'm going to be able to sleep after that game today? And these telegrams…the rumors. Maybe I should call a team meeting…Let them know I'm on to them, that I'll destroy any player who..

GREY: …I don't think you should do that, sir.

COMISKEY: Why not?

GREY: You might end up destroying yourself.

COMISKEY: Destroying myself? What do you mean?

GREY: Maybe this was just one of those games...Or maybe it wasn't.

COMISKEY: If it wasn't, I want to tell them they're going to be ruined. I'll...

GREY: ...They'll be ruined?

COMISKEY: That's right. I'll see to it that they'll be kicked out of the game. Each and every one of the dirty players. They'll never play professional baseball again.

GREY: That may be so, but...

COMISKEY: But what?

GREY: All that valuable property lost.

COMISKEY: You're right...All that property...Th
team might never recover...I might never recover.

GREY: Maybe this was just one of those games. Lik
you've always said, crookedness and baseball don't mi

COMISKEY: You're right, Harry. It's impossible to f
the World Series...I should get some rest. I'm n
myself. I'm not thinking straight.

GREY: You've had a rough day. You can leav
everything to me.

COMISKEY: Thanks. You've lifted my spirits. We'
beat them tomorrow!

(GREY watches his boss as he exits.)

GREY: I'm sure we will, sir...I sure hope we will.

(GREY exits as JOE, LEFTY, CHICK,

KATIE and RING enter.)

RING: The Reds, the first professional team in baseball history, were celebrating their 50th anniversary in 1919. They won the second game of the World Series, beating Joe's best friend, Lefty Williams.

(LEFTY winds up and throws. A loud crack

of the bat is heard as the pitcher mimes

watching the ball fly. He looks at CHICK,

who nods approvingly.)

Joe got three hits, including a double.

(JOE swings as KATIE cheers.

CHICK crosses to LEFTY as

JOE, KATIE and RING exit.)

CHICK: Nice job, Lefty.

LEFTY: Thanks. When'm I gonna get paid for my lack of efforts?

CHICK: I hear ya. I got a meetin' tonight.

LEFTY: Look out fer Joe, too, will ya?

CHICK: I don't know. He got three hits today.

LEFTY: He's with us.

CHICK: Ya sure? Don't seem like he's with us.

LEFTY: He's with us. Lettin' us use his name. I know 'cause I'm representin' him...kind of.

(LEFTY exits as SLEEPY BILLY enters.)

CHICK: When the fuck are we gonna get our money, Billy?

SLEEPY BILLY: Watch yer language. Relax. Y'all get your money in due time.

118

CHICK: In due time? What the fuck's that supposed to mean?

SLEEPY BILLY: All right, all right. I was just playin' with ya.

CHICK: Ya better not play around with me, Billy, ya know I'm not the kinda guy ya can fuck with.

SLEEPY BILLY: (*Hands Chick an envelope.*) This should shut that potty mouth of yers.

CHICK: How much's in there? Sure don't look like no 80 grand.

SLEEPY BILLY: Look at it as an installment. Ten big ones.

CHICK: Ten grand. Eight players. Ya really think that's enough to keep us from feelin' like we been double-crossed?

119

SLEEPY BILLY: You gotta be patient. Y'er gonna ge
what ya been promised.

CHICK: Patient!? Ya expect me to tell 'em to be
patient?

SLEEPY BILLY: Yeah, I do. Didn't your mother teacl
ya?

CHICK: What?

SLEEPY BILLY: Patience's a virtue. See ya 'round.

(SLEEPY BILLY exits.)

CHICK: BASTARD!

(JOE and RING enter.)

RING: Game Three surprised everyone when rookie Dickey Kerr shut out the Reds. Joe continued his torrid hitting, going two for three.

JOE: (*Talks to Betsy.*) Five hits in two games. Still think I might be tankin', Betsy? Yeah, it was fun. Winnin's a whole lot better'n losin'.

(CHICK swings.)

Even Gandil knocked in a pair. Maybe he's gettin' tired of losin', too.

(JOE and RING exit as the FANS and SLEEPY BILLY enter.)

FAN 1: One day it's milk and honey.

FAN 2: Next day hustlin' 'round for money.

FAN 1: Ev'ry gamblin' man he knows.

FAN 2: Easy come and easy goes.

SLEEPY BILLY: Chick, what the fuck!? Ya cost me
bundle!

CHICK: Watch yer potty mouth, Billy. I told ya w
wasn't happy.

SLEEPY BILLY: Ya gotta trust me, Chick. Haven't
always come through for ya in the past?

CHICK: This ain't a 50 bucks here, 20 bucks kind
thing. We're on the big stage now. Stop fuckin' with u
We was promised 80 grand.

SLEEPY BILLY: Stop fuckin' with me! Y'all get y
money.

CHICK: When?

SLEEPY BILLY: Y'all get it if ya lose tomorrow.

CHICK: How much?

SLEEPY BILLY: Twenty g's at least. The rest if ya continue to lose.

CHICK: All right. We'll give ya one more chance.

SLEEPY BILLY: Ya better, or y'er not gettin' another dime outta me or anyone else, guys more powerful'n me, who'll be mighty upset if they feel they been betrayed.

(SLEEPY BILLY exits followed by

CHICK as JOE and RING enter.)

RING: Eddie Cicotte started Game Four and pitched very well after the first game debacle. But in the 5th inning he threw wildly to first base, allowing the runner to advance to scoring position. Jackson fielded a single and made one of his perfect throws to the plate that was deflected by Cicotte, allowing the runner to score.

(JOE fields and throws. He kicks the ground

in disgust as his throw is deflected.)   123

RING: The Reds won 2-0 and were now up in the Series, 3 games to 1.

(SLEEPY BILLY and CHICK

enter as JOE and RING exit.)

SLEEPY BILLY: (*Hands Chick an envelope.*) There ya go. Twenty g's. Ya happy now?

CHICK: I been worse.

SLEEPY BILLY: Divide the dough among your friends'n let 'em know there'll be 20 grand more tomorrow if they're honest…with me.

(CHICK and BILLY exit as

RING and LEFTY enter.)

RING: Game Five was scoreless through five when the Cinci pitcher, Hod Eller, hit a ball between Jackson and the Sox center fielder, Happy Felsch.

124

*(LEFTY winds up, throws, then
watches the flight of a well hit
ball. JOE enters from SR as
HAPPY FELSCH enters SL.)*

JOE: *(Stops and bows.)* After you, Alphonse.

HAPPY: *(Stops and bows.)* After you, Gaston.

*(The ball falls between them.
LEFTY puts his glove over
his face to conceal his
laughter.)*

RING: Felsch made a bad throw that enabled Eller to make it all the way to third. He later scored and the Reds went on to win 5-0. The White Sox had not scored in 22 innings, as Joe's friend Lefty Williams lost his second game. The Series was the best of nine in 1919 so the Reds were just one victory away from the championship.

125

(LEFTY crosses to JOE as RING

and FELSCH exit.)

LEFTY: Nice game, Joe.

JOE: Weren't no nice game. We got beat plain'n simple

LEFTY: Way Hap'n ya let Eller's ball drop between y'all. Hilarious.

JOE: I didn't let nuttin' drop. It was Felsch's ball. He' the captain of the outfield. I always played to win since I first put on this uniform.

LEFTY: And that uni o' yourn's lookin' mighty dirty Comiskey's too cheap to get it cleaned. No wonder othe teams call us the Black Sox. See ya later, my friend.

(JOE watches LEFTY exit. He then exit

slowly as SWEDE and CHICK, who is

carrying a bat, enter.)

CHICK: What's wrong with ya, Swede?   Ya ain't yerself.

SWEDE: Thought ya said we'd get another 20 grand if we lost the fifth game. What gives?

CHICK: How the hell do I know? Maybe we're bein' played.

SWEDE: We gotta try to win till they cough up the dough. We lose one more, the Series is over and they won't give us another dime.

CHICK: We gotta put the fear'a God in 'em. We win a couple they'll be shittin' their pants thinkin' we're stickin' it to 'em.

(RING enters.)

RING: The Sox won Game Six with Chick driving in the winning run in the top of the 10th.

(CHICK swings and is congratulated b

SWEDE. RISBERG and RING exit as

SLEEPY BILLY enters.)

SLEEPY BILLY: Y'er gonna give me a heart attac
Gandil. I thought the Series would be over by now.

CHICK: It woulda been over if ya'd done right by us.

SLEEPY BILLY: Aw c'mon, ya know ya can trust m

CHICK: Sure I trust ya…'bout as far as I can throw y
Ya promised another 20 grand after another loss. We g
nuttin' after the fifth game. You gotta stop fuckin' wi
us. The players are pissed.

SLEEPY BILLY: No, you'n yer pissed pals gotta st
fuckin' around! There're others much bigger'n me wl
are in on this.

CHICK: Like who?

SLEEPY BILLY: Ya don't wanna know, but ya don't wanna make 'em mad if ya know what's good for ya.

CHICK: Get us the money'n they'll get what they want.

(SLEEPY BILLY and CHICK exit as RING and JOE enter.)

RING: Cicotte pitched brilliantly in Game Seven, the first he actually tried to win. Shoeless Joe got two more hits and drove in a pair.

(JOE swings Black Betsy.)

JOE: *(Talks to his bat.)* We win tomorrow Betsy'n the Series is all tied up. Two wins in a row! Seems like even the crooked players bin playin' like they're wantin' us to win. Y'er right. Maybe they come to thur senses'n realize what they bin doin's wrong.

(RING and JOE exit as SLEEPY BILLY and CHICK enter.)

129

SLEEPY BILLY: Yer makin' a big mistake if ya think you can get away with a double-cross.

CHICK: Ya been double-crossin' us. Y'er gettin' yer own back.

SLEEPY BILLY: Chick, we been friends…

CHICK: Associates.

SLEEPY BILLY: Ok, associates…for years. I don't wanna see anything bad happen to ya.

CHICK: Like what?

SLEEPY BILLY: Use yer imagination…and multiply that by 10. That'll give ya an idea of what might happen. The higher-ups…

CHICK: Jus' who're these higher-ups? Who're these guys?

SLEEPY BILLY: Guys like Arnold fuckin' Rothstein, that's who.

CHICK: Rothstein?

SLEEPY BILLY: And others who've killed for less.

CHICK: Ya gotta do more'n make cheap threats.

SLEEPY BILLY: Like I said, y'all get yer money.

CHICK: When and how?

SLEEPY BILLY: Forty grand in the Hotel Warner safe …After ya lose the Series.

CHICK: After the Series? That means never. Why should we trust you?

SLEEPY BILLY: Ya got no choice.

CHICK: We gotta choice. We can keep on winnin'.

SLEEPY BILLY: You win the Series'n y'er gonna be
lookin' over yer shoulder the rest of yer fuckin' life. And
not only you…

CHICK: Whaddya mean?

SLEEPY BILLY: Yer families, ya dumb fuck! Yer
wives…yer children. Ain't none of 'em gonna be safe.
Why take the risk when I'm promisin' ya 40 grand? And
ya can divide it up any way ya want. Keep most of it for
yerself, I don't give a shit.

CHICK: We'll lose, but if the money's not there, it's
you gonna need to be lookin' over yer shoulder.

*(SLEEPY BILLY exits as LEFTY enters
and confronts CHICK.)*

LEFTY: The deal was I'd get 10 grand before the last
game.

CHICK: Don't worry, you'll get yer money. What difference does it make if ya get it a little later than expected?

LEFTY: I'm gonna win tomorrow. I'm sick of bein' fucked over.

CHICK: Don't do anything stupid, Lefty! Don't mess around with these gamblers.

LEFTY: Jus' who're "these gamblers"? Y'er the only one who's had any kinda dealin' with 'em. I'd like to meet one of 'em face-to-face.

CHICK: No, you wouldn't! Don't play hardball with these guys. Play along. Lose tomorrow'n the Series is over. You'll get yer money. I guarantee it.

LEFTY: Y'all guarantee it? What the fuck's that supposed to mean? Why should I trust ya? How do I know they ain't been givin' ya money'n y'er keepin' it all yerself?

(CHICK grabs LEFTY

SLEEPY BILLY enters

CHICK: Listen to me! Y'er gonna lose tomorrow so p
yer double-crossin' thoughts outta yer head!

(CHICK shoves LEFTY and exit

LEFTY turns and is facing

SLEEPY BILLY.)

SLEEPY BILLY: Why, if it isn't Claude "Lefty
Williams, star southpaw of the Chicago White Sox!
sure is an honor and a pleasure to make yo
acquaintance.

LEFTY: Whaddya want?

SLEEPY BILLY: Why Mr. Williams, I'm just a f
thrilled to meet one of his heroes.

LEFTY: WHADDYA WANT!?

SLEEPY BILLY: Don't raise your voice to me.

(LEFTY tries to get by, but

is stopped by BILLY.)

I saw your wife at the game today, Mr. Claude "Lefty" Williams. My, she sure is a pretty little…thing. It'd be terrible if somethin' happened to mar those attractive features…

LEFTY: Whaddya mean ya little prick?!

(LEFTY shoves BILLY, who reaches

in his coat for a gun.)

SLEEPY BILLY: I think ya know exactly what I mean, and I think ya know what I expect ya to do to see your pretty little wife stays pretty.

LEFTY: I know.

SLEEPY BILLY: I thought ya might need some further instructions…specific instructions.

135

LEFTY: Like what?

SLEEPY BILLY: Don't play around. I want Cinci to jump out front early. The Series must end tomorrow. Got it?

LEFTY: *(Softly.)* Got it.

SLEEPY BILLY: What's that? Couldn't hear ya.

LEFTY: I GOT IT!!!

SLEEPY BILLY: Why, Mr. Williams, it's refreshing to find out how very cooperative ya are. It's a pleasure doin' business with a man like you.

LEFTY: I GOT IT ALL RIGHT!

SLEEPY BILLY: The first inning! The first inning should be all Cincinnati!

(LEFTY starts to exit.)

136

SLEEPY BILLY: Oh, Mr. Williams, would you mind giving me your autograph? My kid's your biggest fan.

> *(LEFTY exits angrily. SLEEPY turns*
>
> *and faces the entering RING.)*

Look who's here! Why if it isn't the star reporter for the Chicago Tribune!

> *(RING starts to exit.)*

Would ya like to make a small wager on the game?

RING: Not interested.

SLEEPY BILLY: C'mon, it'll make the game more intrestin'.

RING: I said I'm not interested.

SLEEPY BILLY: Take it from me. A bet on Cinci's like money in the bank.

RING: Why do you say that?

SLEEPY BILLY: You'll be able to go home early. It'l
be over after the first inning. See ya 'round...Mr
"Professional Fan."

(SLEEPY exits as JOE enters.)

RING: In Game Eight, Williams managed to get the firs
batter to pop out, but the next four got hits and eventually
scored. Joe had another great game going 2-for-5 anc
driving in three. He hit the only home run in the Series.

(JOE swings. A loud crack of the

bat is heard as the crowd cheers.)

The slugger just missed another homer flying out to deep
center field.

(JOE swings. The crowd cheers

then groans.)

Final score, the Reds 10 and the White Sox 5.

(JOE exits as RING crosse

to the entering KID.)

RING: Say, Kid, got any comment for the press about losing the Series?

KID: Why don't ya talk to the Reds' manager? He won. He'll be glad to talk to ya.

RING: We gotta get the view from the losing side, too, Kid. The fans expect it.

KID: I could talk to ya about this here Series. Yeah, there's plenty I could tell.

RING: Like what?

KID: Never ya mind...No, I'll tell ya what. Ya can write in yer column that seven players won't be reportin' to the Sox trainin' camp next season. Not if I have anything to say about it.

RING: Thanks for the scoop, Kid.

(RING exits as CHICK and

SWEDE enter.)

KID: Congratulations, Gandil.   You had a helluv
Series.

CHICK: Congratulations to you, too, Kid, you ol' so
of a....

(KID lunges at CHICK, tryir

to strangle him. He is pulle

off CHICK by SWEDE.)

It's been a real pleasure workin' with ya, Kid. It breal
my heart to tell ya I've decided to retire.

KID: Whaddya talkin' about?

CHICK: I think ya heard me, Kid. I been savin' n
pennies so I don't think I'll have to worry 'bout worki
for a while. It sure was nice havin' a generous employ
like Mr. Charles Comiskey so I could take an ear
retirement.

1⁴

KID: Ya go to hell!

CHICK: It's been nice knowin' ya, too, Kid. Let's go get us a drink to celebrate, Swede.

(Starts to exit. Stops.)

And ya can tell Mr. Comiskey I'm done bein' his property…And I sure as hell won't be goin' back to the coal mines.

(BLACKOUT. LIGHTS UP on CHICK,

LEFTY and SWEDE at a local bar.

CHICK hands LEFTY a dirty

envelope.)

CHICK: There ya go. Ten grand. Five fer you'n five fer Joe. Ya earned it. Losin' three games'n Joe fer lettin' us use his name with the gamblers.

LEFTY: Five grand? I was promised ten.

141

CHICK: Yeah, well, some got promised more'n got paid less. Those damn gamblers pulled a double-cross on us.

LEFTY: I ain't never played to lose before. That game, the last one, felt like it took 'bout nine hours.

CHICK: Don't worry 'bout it. The Series is over, that's all that matters.

LEFTY: Over? It won't ever be over.

CHICK: Whaddya mean?

LEFTY: It's gonna stay with me. In my dreams. I had this here dream. I'm pitchin' the way I always used to. Puttin' all I got into ev'ry throw. But the catcher, he misses ev'ry ball. Not 'cause he can't catch it, but 'cause he don't want to. And the fielders, they let ev'ry ball go through, ev'ry fly drop. And it goes on and on…and on. I keep lookin' at the bullpen, hopin', prayin' Kid'll warm somebody up. Take me out. But he don't. And there ain't no end…'Cause there's never any outs. And I got to stay out there pitchin' my heart out. Forever…forever losin'.   142

CHICK: Don't worry 'bout that. Those bad dreams'll stop soon's ya go on that vacation yer wife's been beggin' ya to take her on.

LEFTY: Vacation? I'm sure needin' a vacation.

CHICK: And think of all that fine jewelry ya can buy her.

LEFTY: The kind Comiskey's wife always wears?

CHICK: Yeah, the kind Mrs. Fat-Fuckin'-Commy always wears.

LEFTY: What about the fans?

CHICK: What about 'em?

LEFTY: The way we let 'em all down.

CHICK: Fuck 'em. Sure the bugs'll be behind ya when we're goin' good, but they'll turn on ya ev'ry time. 143

LEFTY: Y'er right. I seen it. I seen it happen plenty o
times.

SWEDE: We all seen it.

>*(BLACKOUT. LIGHTS UP on*
>*LEFTY, holding a dirty envelope*
>*as he confronts JOE.)*

LEFTY: Take it, Joe!

JOE: What the hell's that?

LEFTY: It's yer share...From Gandil.

JOE: My share of what? What the hell come off here?

LEFTY: Y'er a part of this thing whether ya wanna be
or not.

JOE: I ain't no part of nuttin'.   14

LEFTY: I told him ya was.

JOE: Told who?

LEFTY: Gandil. I told Gandil.

JOE: I never told ya could tell that bastard nuttin'. Why'd ya wanna go'n do that for?

LEFTY: I'm yer friend. I was lookin' out fer ya.

JOE: Lookin' out?

LEFTY: I wanted ya to make some money, too. Ya earned it.

JOE: Earned it? Anybody watchin' the Series could see I done my best to win.

LEFTY: It was fer the use of yer name, damn it! The gamblers wouldn't've put up a cent less'n they thought you was part of the fix. So I told Chick ya was.   145

JOE: You shouldn't a done that.   I didn't give ya ı
permission to do that.

LEFTY: There's 5,000 dollars in this here envelope, Jo
There shoulda been more, but them lousy gamblers, the
done us a double-cross.

JOE: I don't care 'bout no double-cross. I don't wa
yer money.

LEFTY: Take it, Joe!

> *(LEFTY throws the money at JOI*
>
> *feet and starts to exit.)*

JOE: (*Picks up envelope.*) I'll take it, all right. Fir
thing tomorrow, I'm takin' it to Comiskey'n tellin' hi
all 'bout this.

> *(LEFTY stops and looks at JO*
>
> *for a moment then exits. JO*
>
> *puts the envelope in his*
>
> *pocket as KATIE enters.)*   1

KATIE: What happened?   What were you'n Lefty arguin' 'bout?

JOE: We wasn't arguin'.

KATIE: You were shoutin' at each other like I never heard before.

JOE: We was havin' a…disagreement.

KATIE: A disagreement? 'Bout what?

(*JOE shows her the envelope.*)

JOE: This.

KATIE: What's that?

JOE: What's it look like? It's a dirty envelope.

KATIE: What's in it? 147

JOE: Dirty money. Dirty money in a goddamn dirty envelope.

KATIE: Dirty money? Why's Lefty givin' ya money?

JOE: He wants me to be part of somethin'.

KATIE: Part of what?

JOE: Somethin' dirty…I'm not tellin' ya no more.

KATIE: Joe, I'm yer wife. I gotta right to know.

JOE: They wanna drag me in on their scheme, but I weren't no part of it.

KATIE: Scheme? What kinda scheme?

JOE: Throwin' games.

KATIE: Throwin' games? Lefty's been throwin' games?

JOE: Lefty'n some of them others.

KATIE: Others? Who else's been throwin' games?

JOE: All of 'em! Some of 'em! Dunno how many.

KATIE: What an awful thing to do. So, what're we gonna do?

JOE: I told Williams that I was gonna tell Comiskey... Maybe I should jus' keep it.

KATIE: Keep it?

JOE: If'n I tell on 'em...Gandil...Risberg...they're dangerous men...the gamblers, too. They could come after us.

KATIE: We can't keep that money, Joe.

JOE: Lefty says I earned it.

KATIE: How'd ya earn it? Were ya throwin' games too?

JOE: No! Ya been at all the games. I been playin' the best ball of my life this Series. No one could possibly think I was playin' to lose. But I still earned it.

KATIE: How?

JOE: Fer the use of my name.

KATIE: Use of yer name?

JOE: Lefty says the gamblers wouldn't have put up a cent if I weren't no part of it.

KATIE: We can't keep this money, Joe.

*(JOE takes the cash out of
the envelope and shows it to
KATIE, who slowly touches
it, then pulls her hand back
as if she had felt an electric
shock.)*

JOE: I could buy ya an awful lot of nice things, Katie. Jus' like I promised. Way I figure. We deserve it.

KATIE: Deserve it?

JOE: Isn't that why ya wanted me to play ball…to make as much money as I can? Any way I can.

KATIE: Not this way…Not this way. That'd be wrong.

JOE: What's so wrong about it? Ya know what's wrong? What's wrong's the way it's the bosses who always get rich off the backs of their workers. Ain't that what we always believed? That's what's wrong.

KATIE: What's really wrong's the team deliberate
losin' when they shoulda been playin' their hearts out
win. Think of yer fans. The way they live'n die with tl
team. It's nuttin' but a betrayal. Ya should do what y
told Lefty ya was gonna do.

JOE: What's that?

KATIE: Take it to Comiskey. Show him the money'ı
tell him what's been goin' on.

(BLACKOUT. LIGHTS UP on CHIC.
GANDIL sitting in the waiting roo
of COMISKEY'S office as JOE enter

JOE: Chick.

CHICK: Joe. Thought you'd be headin' on home
Georgia by now.

JOE: I'll be goin' later. Can't get outta here fast enoug

CHICK: I hear ya…What're ya…

JOE: A helluva lotta of scandal goin' 'round fer what had happened.

CHICK: To hell with it.

(Grey enters and crosses to Chick.)

GREY: Mr. Comiskey is ready to see you now.

(CHICK exits as GREY turns on JOE.)

What do you want?!

JOE: I'm wantin' to see the Boss.

GREY: About what?

(JOE shows him the envelope with the cash.)

JOE: 'Bout this. Tell the Boss I gotta see him. It's 'bout Williams.

GREY: The Boss can't see you now, Joe.

JOE: Ya don't understand.

GREY: No, you don't understand! The Boss will not see you today!

JOE: But it's *real* impor…

GREY: GO HOME, JOE! We know what you want.

(GREY turns on his heels and exits.
JOE stares in his direction for a
moment then slowly exits.)

(BLACKOUT. LIGHTS UP on
JOE and KATIE preparing to
return home for the off-season.)

JOE: So, whadda we gonna do now?   154

KATIE: We're gonna finish up our packin' and head on home just like we do at the end of every season.

JOE: Ain't never been a season like this.

KATIE: We gotta put it outta our minds'n get on with our lives. That's all we can do, honey.

JOE: Maybe I should try'n see Comiskey again before we leave. Grey slammed the door in my face, but maybe the Boss'd see me now.

KATIE: I'm beginnin' to think they don't wanna know, Joe. Or they know what's been goin' on and they're not gonna do nothin' 'bout it.

JOE: Why'd they do that?

KATIE: I don't know'n right now I don't really care. I gave up long ago tryin' to figure these Yankees out. I think we should get our business goin', get outta baseball'n get away from these people as soon as we can.

155

JOE: I feel sorry fer the fans. I heard some of 'em los
their life savin's bettin' on us. Maybe I shoulda warnec
'em.

KATIE: Ya couldn't do that, Joe. They're dangerou:
men, those gamblers. Lyria Williams told me the)
threatened to hurt her if Lefty won the last game. W
jus' gotta try'n forget this ever happened, at least fo
now, and get on with our lives.

JOE: I don't know that I'll ever forget this happened
And what about this?

(He shows her the envelope with the money.

KATIE: Put that dirty money away.

JOE: Where?

KATIE: Anywhere. Ya can burn it for all I care.

JOE: I ain't gonna burn 5,000 dollars, Katie. What good would that do anybody?

KATIE: I don't care. I wish I never seen it…that ya never showed it to me. Ya should've jus' left it on the floor.

JOE: Fer the cleanin' lady to get? I always try to be a generous tipper, but that woulda bin 'bout 4,000 dollars too much.

KATIE: Maybe you should try'n give it to some fans who lost their savin's on the Series…I don't know…C'mon, let's finish our packin' and head on home.

(*BLACKOUT.*)

(*LIGHTS UP on a courtroom. A JUDGE holding a gavel sits on the bench.*)

JUDGE: Next case!

(*A FAN wearing long johns enters. He is cuffed with his hands covering his crotch.*) 157

JUDGE: It says here that you are negligent with yo[u]
alimony and child support payments. How do y[ou]
plead?

FAN: Guilty, Your Honor.

JUDGE: I see that your payment record has be[en]
spotless up to now. I hate to send a man to alimony j[ail]
unless there's no other recourse. Haven't you the mea[ns]
to make the payments?

FAN: No, Your Honor. The only thing I have in t[he]
world is what I'm holding in my hands right now.

JUDGE: Your record has been so good. Wh[at]
happened?

FAN: Well, if you must know, Your Honor, I lost m[y]
shirt betting on the White Sox.

JUDGE: *(Slams gavel.)* Thirty days! Next case!

(BLACKOUT. LIGHTS UP on

RING who stands at CS.) 15[6]

RING: Baseball's been described as "a game for children played by men for profit." Something so pure, poetic when played by kids. Leave it to men to fuck it up. Men will find a way to corrupt anything if it will make them money. Rumors were rife right after the last pitch that the rotten Series had been thrown.

(RING exits as GREY and COMISKEY enter.)

COMISKEY: My team could be destroyed. We've got to nip the rumors of a fix in the bud. But how?

GREY: You could issue a statement.

COMISKEY: Statement? What kind of statement?

GREY: You could say you're conducting an investigation …that you believe the Series was honestly played. And you could offer a reward.

COMISKEY: Reward for what?

GREY: For information the Series was fixed.

COMISKEY: How much should I offer?

GREY: It has to be substantial, given the gravity of the situation.

COMISKEY: How substantial?

GREY: Twenty thousand. Anyone who knows anything will come to us first, hoping to claim the reward. We'll control whatever evidence is out there.

COMISKEY: Twenty…thousand…dollars? I'm going to destroy my team plus I'm paying twenty thousand dollars to whomever will help me do it!

GREY: You won't have to pay a cent and the team won't be destroyed…So long as we play our cards right.

(GREY and COMISKEY exit as RING

enters holding a newspaper.)   160

RING: Henry Ford famously said, "History is bunk." According to the Library of Congress, more books have been written about Lincoln than any other American, although honest Abe said he rarely read biographies or histories. When asked why, Lincoln said he could never be sure that what he read in books was what really happened. But he did read newspapers.

(RING exits as JOE and KATIE enter.

KATIE holds a newspaper.)

KATIE: The newspaper says Comiskey's offerin' 20,000 dollars for proof there was wrongdoin' durin' the World Series.

JOE: Twenty thousand dollars! There's plenty I could tell 'em.

KATIE: And you should tell, reward or no reward. And Comiskey's written ya a letter, Joe.

JOE: A letter? What's it say?

KATIE: *(Takes out a letter and reads.)* "There has been a great deal of adverse talk in which your name has been mentioned reflecting on your integrity in the recent World Series. Would gladly pay your expenses to Chicago if you wish to come on in reference to the matter pertaining to the talk emanating from the World Series."

JOE: How could my name be mentioned? My playing proved I did all I could to win.

KATIE: Let's write and tell him that.

(KATIE picks up a pen and a piece

of paper as JOE dictates.)

JOE: To Mr. Charles Comiskey. Your letter just came and I sure am surprised to hear that my name has been connected with any scandal in the recent World Series as I think my playing proved that I did all I could to win...I will be only too glad to come to Chicago and clear my name.

(JOE and KATIE exit as COMISKEY and

GREY enter. HARRY reads Joe's letter.) 162

GREY: ..."I did all I could do to win and I think my record for the Series will show if you look at it. Let me hear from you as to when you want me to come to Chicago. Signed, Joe Jackson." What should I do with this?

COMISKEY: File it away!

GREY: Are you going to answer the letter?

COMISKEY: File it away! If the sordid details of this ever got out it could destroy baseball. Without the game, what would I have ever accomplished? Probably would've been a plumber or bricklayer. Baseball gave me the wonderful life I've had. Without it...I can't have the game's destruction on my conscience.

>*(BLACKOUT. LIGHTS UP on JOE and KATIE sitting in their living room. JOE holds the envelope containing the bribe money.)*

KATIE: It's been two weeks. Clearly, Comiskey don't wanna hear yer side of the story.   163

JOE: I could go back to Chicago'n try'n see him, b
Grey'd probably slam the door in my face agai
(*Indicating envelope*) So, what're we gonna do with thi

KATIE: I don't know. Whaddya think we should
with it? Give it back to Lefty?

JOE: I don't want the damn stuff, but since that lou
so-called gamblin' outfit used my name, I might as we
have their money as fer Williams.

KATIE: I'll deposit it in the bank tomorrow. Yer sister
got some surgery comin' up. We can put some of th
dirty money to good use'n help her pay her medical bil

JOE: Sounds good to me.

(*BLACKOUT. LIGHTS UP on COMISKEY*
office. GREY enters carrying a briefcase
COMISKEY sits at his desk.)

GREY: I'm all packed and ready to go...Where am
heading?   1

COMISKEY: Jackson returned his contract unsigned. I want you to go down to Georgia and sign him up for three years.

GREY: Maybe he's upset you didn't answer his letter.

COMISKEY: Don't mention the letter.

GREY: What if he brings it up?

COMISKEY: Just tell him the investigation is complete and we know he wasn't crooked.

GREY: What about the money?

COMISKEY: The money?

GREY: The bribe money…Maybe we should tell him he can keep it.

COMISKEY: Keep it? 165

GREY: It might be better for us...If the story of the Series ever gets out, it'll look bad for Joe if he kept the money. We'll be able to keep him under control.

COMISKEY: Yes, I think you're right. If he implicates himself, we'll make sure he doesn't incriminate us.

GREY: And what about the 10-Day clause? He's not going to want to sign if it's in the contract.

COMISKEY: You don't think I'd offer a three-year contract without it, do you? Don't come back till you have him signed.

(BLACKOUT. LIGHTS UP on

KATIE sweeping her front

porch as GREY enters.)

KATIE: Why, if it isn't Harry Grey! What a delightful surprise.

166

GREY: Yes, Mrs. Jackson, I was passing through Georgia and noticed a light in your window so, I thought I'd drop by for a visit.

KATIE: I never took ya for the "drop by for a visit" type. Isn't Georgia a little outta yer way, say, about a thousand miles?

GREY: I have to admit this isn't just a pleasure visit, Mrs. Jackson. There's a bit of business involved...Joe returned his contract unsigned.

KATIE: We returned it because it was an insult.

GREY: I'm sure Mr. Comiskey will be sorry to hear you feel that way. Perhaps the generous terms he's offering Joe in a new contract will assuage your feelings.

KATIE: We're not easily "assuaged." I'm sure you've brought along a copy for our perusal.

GREY: Why, as a matter of fact, I have.

KATIE: Ya got the nerve to offer Joe a measly two thousand dollar raise!

GREY: We lost the World Series.

KATIE: Ya blamin' that on Joe?

GREY: No, of course not. Joe had a fine Series.

KATIE: A "fine" Series? He set a record! Twelve hits. He made sixteen putouts and no errors.

GREY: Yes, but there are other…problems.

KATIE: What do you mean…"problems"?

GREY: That's something I'd prefer to talk to Joe about.

KATIE: Y'all talk to me.   168

GREY: I think I hear a car pulling up. Could that be…

KATIE: …Joe will be back in a few minutes. Did ya get our letter?

GREY: Letter?

KATIE: Don't play dumb with me, Harry. Ya know what I'm talkin' about. Does the Boss want to hear what Joe has to say or not?

GREY: Mr. Comiskey believes he knows all that he needs to know.

KATIE: More like all he wants to know…Ya might as well head back North because Joe's not signin'. We're very happy and doin' very well with our dry cleanin' business. You can tell Mr. Comiskey we've achieved our goal.

GREY: And what might that be?

KATIE: He needs us more than we need him. Kindly
show yerself out.

> (*KATIE exits. GREY turns*
>
> *leave as JOE enters.*)

GREY: Hiya, Joe!

JOE: Harry Grey…Y'er 'bout the last person I w
hopin'…expectin' to see here in Georgia.

GREY: Yes, I must say that this is a lovely part of t
country…Was that your new car I heard pulling u
Would you mind giving me a lift into town so I ca
admire some more of this beautiful southern scenery?

JOE: Guess it'd be okay.

> (*JOE and GREY sit in two chai*
>
> *as JOE pantomimes driving.*)

Did Comiskey git my letter?

GREY: He got it. Don't worry, Joe, our investigation has been completed.

JOE: I was given 5,000 dollars. They said it was fer the use of my name.

GREY: We know.

JOE: I showed it to ya right after I got it'n you slammed the damn door in my face!...What should I do with it?

GREY: Keep it.

JOE: Really?

GREY: As long as that bunch of bums used your name, you did the only sensible thing in keeping it. And I've got some more good news for you. Mr. Comiskey's offering you a three-year contract raising your salary from six to eight thousand dollars a year!

JOE: A three-year contract and I should keep the bribe money? Katie'n me bin thinkin' on it. Way we figure, a lotta people gonna git hurt if this story blows. I don't wanna be one of 'em.

GREY: It's not going to "blow," Joe. Not if everyone concerned is...careful.

> *(GREY gives him the contract*
>
> *and a pen as JOE stops the car.)*

Don't you want to play baseball, Joe? Don't you want to be a member of the White Sox?

JOE: 'Course I do, Harry, but...

GREY: Listen, Joe, Mr. Comiskey knows you weren't involved in the World Series...problem. That's why he doesn't want to talk to you. He doesn't need to. By signing you again, our star player, we're telling the world that we believe in you. We wouldn't sign a crook to our team. You stick with us and we'll stand by you.

> *(JOE looks at the contract.)*

You're a ballplayer, Joe, not a dry cleaner!

JOE: Ten-Day Clause in it?

GREY: No. We knew you wouldn't sign a contract that contains the 10-Day Clause. Mr. Comiskey wants to do all he can to prove that we're behind you.

JOE: It's a three-year contract. Eight thousand a year…

GREY: …That's right, 8,000 and no 10-Day Clause, Joe. A raise and a three-year contract because we appreciate your loyalty to the organization.

JOE: I'll sign it, Harry, if ya shake my hand and tell me it's true.

GREY: *(He shakes JOE'S hand.)* May lightning strike me dead if this isn't true.

> *(JOE signs. BLACKOUT. LIGHTS UP on*
> *RING and FANS sitting in the stands*
> *at a baseball park.)*

RING: 1920. The dead ball was replaced by the live ball ushering in the age of the home run. The White Sox, Yankees and Indians were locked in one of the most exciting pennant races in the history of the game. Meanwhile, a Chicago grand jury investigating a suspicious Cubs game decided to turn its attention to all those rumors about the 1919 World Series.

FAN 1: If the Sox win today, they'll be one game out with only four to go!

RING: Some pennant race, huh?

FAN 2: The Sox'll win it.

FAN 1: The Indians and Yankees ain't got a chance.

RING: New York's got the Babe.

FAN 2: I'll take Shoeless over Ruth any day.

FAN 2: Williams, Cicotte, Faber…

FAN 1: …and Kerr. All got 20 wins on one team!

FAN 2: That's never been done before!

RING: If you guys could hear yourselves. Buncha jamooks.

FAN 1: You talkin' to me?

RING: Why don't you go see something that's on the level? I hear there's a wrestling match uptown.

FAN 2: Whaddya talkin' about?

> *(JOE enters and stands at home*
> *plate at CS.)*

RING: I helped make Joe Jackson the mythical figure he is today.

FAN 1: Yeah, and I shot McKinley.

RING: The grand jury's conducting an investigation.

FAN 1: Investigation? About what?

RING: Last year's World Series.

FAN 2: We blew it last year, but not this…

                    (*JOE swings and hits a home run*

FAN 1: A home run!

FAN 2: Joe's battin' average is over .380!

RING: The Series was fixed.

FAN 2: Fixed? They tried to lose?

RING: That's right. And Jackson's been named as one
of the crooked players.

(The stunned FANS react to the news.)

FAN 1: Jackson, you're a crook!

FAN 2: They should put ya in jail, ya bum!

(The FANS exit as SWEDE enters and crosses to JOE.)

JOE: What the hell's goin' on?

SWEDE: Got some bad news, Joe. Cicotte's squealin'.

JOE: Squealin'? 'Bout what?

SWEDE: Whaddya think? Ya better not talk, Jackson. I'll kill ya if you squawk!

(JOE and SWEDE exit. RING takes a drink and starts to exit. He is stopped by the entering SLEEPY BILLY.)   177

SLEEPY BILLY: Where ya goin', Lardner? Ya ain't leavin', are ya?

RING: Get outta my way!

SLEEPY BILLY: You hate my guts, don't ya?

RING: (*Drinks from his flask.*) Billy, at this moment, I hate everybody's guts.

SLEEPY BILLY: Ya better lay off the booze, my friend.

RING: (*Takes another drink.*) Thanks for the advice.

SLEEPY BILLY: I'm willin' to bet every dollar I made on the 1919 Series...You'll be back.

RING: I wish you'd bet every dollar you won on the fix, because it's one bet you'd lose.

SLEEPY BILLY: You'll be there, Lard-butt. It's the Great American Game. 178

RING: Baseball. HA!

(SLEEPY BILLY exits as two FANS enter.)

FAN 1: Whenever I'm sad…

FAN 2: And the world's treatin' me bad.

FAN 1: Into some rathskeller I stray.

FAN 2: I fill up a stein…

FAN 1: With this old friend of mine.

FAN 2: And I dream all my sorrows away.

(RING and the FANS exit as COMISKEY, JOE and GREY enter.)

179

COMISKEY: To Eddie Cicotte, Charles Risberg, Fred McMullin, Joe Jackson, Oscar Felsch, George Weaver and Claude Williams…You and each of you are hereby notified of your indefinite suspension as a member of the Chicago White Sox baseball club. Your suspension is brought about by information which has just come to me directly involving you and each of you in the baseball scandal resulting from the World Series of 1919.

JOE: But I tried to tell ya!

COMISKEY: If you are innocent of any wrongdoing you and each of you will be reinstated.

JOE: I'm innocent. Grey said ya know I weren't no part of it.

COMISKEY: If you are guilty, you will be retired from organized baseball for the rest of your lives, if I can accomplish it.

JOE: Ya wouldn't listen…Ya didn't wanna know.

COMISKEY: Until there is a finality to this investigation, it is due to the public that I take this action, even though it costs Chicago the pennant.

(COMISKEY collapses as JOE exits. The owner is helped off by GREY as LEFTY, SWEDE and CHICK enter.)

LEFTY: Poor Commy.

SWEDE: Yeah, my heart bleeds for him.

CHICK: Let's give FFC a sailor's farewell. "Goodbye, good luck and to hell with ya!"

LEFTY: I guess ya outsmarted everybody again, gettin' outta baseball before this thing blew up.

CHICK: The secret of success in anything is timin'. Baseball taught me that. Timin'. When to swing; when to hold up; when to stay put; when to run.

SWEDE: Yeah, Chick, I gotta hand it to ya. Ya su
was persuasive.

LEFTY: Ya sure was. And ya know, the funny thing
I can't really remember tellin' ya I'd go along with tl
fix...I probably did, but it seems more like I jus' let
happen.

SWEDE: It seemed so easy...

LEFTY: ...So damned easy...

CHICK: (*Leafing through a wad of cash.*) ...Soooo eas

(*LEFTY angrily slams down his baseball glove*

LEFTY: What'm I gonna do? Go to hell, I guess. I g
5,000 dollars. I woulda got that much if the Sox ha
won. And now I'm outta baseball. Thrown out. Becau
I was crooked. Have I gained anything? We've so
ourselves and our jobs, the only job we know anythin
about. We've gotten in return only a few bucks, while
buncha gamblers have gotten rich. The joke's on us. 1

(CHICK slowly picks up LEFTY's glove and hands it to the pitcher.)

CHICK: Yeah, it is kinda funny.

(The three players look at each other glumly for a moment and then burst out laughing. The next section of the scene is stylized.)

SWEDE: Ah, remember the third game, the one we really tried to win?

CHICK: (*Excessively polite.*) No, Swede, pardon me, but I believe you're mistaken. Yes, I know you're quite mistaken. It was the fourth game.

LEFTY: No, excuse me, gentlemen, it pains me to correct you, yes, it hurts me to correct you, but I know it was the fifth game.

SWEDE: And the catch you made,

In that third game.

It really was remarkable,

So very, very remarkable.

CHICK: That catch, dear Swede,

Though extraordinary,

Yes, quite extraordinary,

Was in the fourth, not third.

Of this, I am quite certain,

So very, very certain.

LEFTY: Oh, gentlemen, I remember that play,

In the fifth inning of the fifth game.

Yes, Chick, you were magnificent.

So very, very magnificent.

CHICK: No, sirs, I know, I made the play!

In the fourth inning of the fourth game.

Two men were out, a mighty clout,

Did in my glove remain.   184

SWEDE: No, Chick, that play so extraordinaire,

Was the third inning of the third game.

CHICK: It was the fourth, you slimy Swede.

LEFTY: Now, Chick, let's not get personal.

That last remark,

You must admit,

It really was quite personal.

So very, very personal.

SWEDE: Keep out of this, you son of a bitch,

If I want your opinion, I'll ask for it.

I will most certainly ask for it.

(SWEDE shoves LEFTY.)

LEFTY: Now, Swede, let's not get physical,

You must refrain from getting physical.

(LEFTY pushes SWEDE.)   185

CHICK: I'm glad I quit,

So glad I quit,

To get away from you two.

You are a stupid duo,

A very stupid duo.

(LEFTY and SWEDE pounce on

CHICK.)

LEFTY: It was the fifth!

SWEDE: It was the third!

CHICK: It was the fourth!

(They fight. Stylized section ends.

CHICK: C'mon, you guys, let's cut this crap!

SWEDE: Yeah, sorry, Chick...Lefty. I don't know what got into me.

LEFTY: It's funny how things happen, y'know.

CHICK: Well, let's forget it. We just lost our heads for a second. No harm done. After all, we gotta stick together.

LEFTY: That's right. Stick this out together.

CHICK: Yeah...Well, it's good to see you guys again...Take it easy.

(CHICK exits SR.)

LEFTY: Yeah, take care of yerself.

(LEFTY exits SL.)

SWEDE: Say, Chick! Can I have a ride in yer new car?

(Sound effect of car driving off is
heard as SWEDE is left alone on stage

(BLACKOUT. LIGHTS UP on
COMISKEY and GREY standing at the
owner's desk.)

COMISKEY: Jackson's waiting to see me. What do
do if he tells the grand jury about the letter he wro
offering to tell me all he knew about the Series?

GREY: Leave me alone with him, sir. I think I ca
convince him not to say anything that could harm you

COMISKEY: Or that he asked to be suspended befo
the Series started? I'll be ruined.

GREY: Leave him to me.

(COMISKEY exits. JOE enters.)

JOE: Is the Boss here?

GREY: The Boss is busy, Joe.

JOE: Seems like he's always too busy whenever I come around…I didn't have nuttin' to do with the Series fix.

GREY: Cicotte says you did.

JOE: I don't know why he would say that.

GREY: You don't?

JOE: Maybe it was somethin' Lefty said to him.

GREY: Why would Lefty have said anything?

JOE: Usin' my name…Without my permission.

GREY: You did take 5,000 dollars from Williams, Joe. You're involved.

JOE: I didn't take it. Williams threw it on the floor and I picked it up'n I tried to tell ya 'bout that money.

GREY: I don't remember.

JOE : I tried to tell ya and ya slammed the door in my face! And I didn't want to play in that damn Series. I asked the Boss to suspend me. Don't you know 'bout that, neither? And the letter I wrote Comiskey...

GREY: Nobody's gonna believe you, Joe.

JOE: I come here for advice. Is the organization gonna stand by me like ya said? Y'er startin' to sound a whole lot different than when we talked down in Georgia.

GREY: That was Georgia. This is Chicago. There's a big difference.

JOE: Way I figure it, a man oughta stand by his word no matter if he says it in Georgia, Chicago or the North Pole. Maybe I'll head on over to that grand jury. I figure I

JOE : (*cont.*) might have a thing or two to tell 'em that they might find intrestin'. What Cicotte said ain't nuttin' compared to what I gotta say.

GREY: Wait, Joe! Of course we're going to stand by you. I apologize if I didn't make myself clear about that. You know Mr. Comiskey's going to do all he can to keep you on his team. You don't think he wants to lose his best player, do you? You certainly don't want to say or do anything that would make the Boss look bad.

(GREY picks up a telephone and dials.)

JOE: Ya said it's not lookin' good fer me. It's gonna look a whole lot worse fer Mr. Fat-Fuckin'-Commy after I get a few things offa my chest. After I tell 'em 'bout that letter I sent...

GREY: I got Judge McDonald from the grand jury on the line, Joe. Anything you want to tell him?

JOE: There's plenty I wanna tell him.

(Joe takes the phone and sits.)

Hello, Judge McDonald?...Joe Jackson.   191

JUDGE: *(Voice.)* What do you want, Jackson?

JOE: You gotta control this thing. I'm an honest man.

JUDGE: *(Voice.)* I know, Jackson, that you are not.

JOE: But Judge, if you'll jus' listen, there's plenty could tell.

JUDGE: *(Voice.)* Don't tell me over the phone. Tell me in court.

(The JUDGE hangs up as JOE stands, stunned.)

GREY: See that, Joe. No one will believe you.

JOE: All I want is to tell my story'n go home. I wanna tell the truth.

GREY: The truth won't be believed, Joe. The Judge doesn't believe you and no one else will either. You could end up in jail.

JOE: So what'm I supposed to do?

GREY: Cooperate. Say you were part of the plot and that you're ashamed of yourself. The gamblers will be furious if they find out you took their money and weren't part of the fix. They can make a person disappear.

JOE: They'd come after me?

GREY: And Katie too…We'll take care of you, Joe. Mr. Comiskey and I will protect you. We don't want you or Katie to get hurt. We're your friends. But you must not say anything that could make Mr. Comiskey look bad. If you do, we won't be able to protect you or Katie.

JOE: I dunno, Harry. I don't feel good lyin' like that, sayin' I was part of that dirty business.

GREY: But you are a part of it, Joe.

JOE: I ain't!

GREY: You are! You kept the bribe money. You pu[t] it in the bank.

JOE: I didn't know what else to do with it. Kat[e] deposited it durin' December. We'd been holdin' it f[or] two months. I woulda brought it back to Chicago [in] November to show Comiskey the dirty envelope with t[he] cash if you'da answered my letter. You told me whe[n I] signed the contract, I should keep it.

GREY: But we didn't say you should spend it.

JOE: Spend it?

GREY: That's right, Joe, we know you've been maki[ng] withdrawals.

JOE: To pay my sister's medical bills. Ain't used t[he] money fer nuttin' else.

GREY: It doesn't matter what the money was used fo[r.] All that will matter is that you took the dirty money a[nd] put it in the bank and then spent it.   1[9]

JOE: I didn't want that dirty money. I wanted to show it to ya...I wanted...So what should I do?

GREY: Say you were part of it. You took the money. Gandil was the instigator. You tried to lose.

JOE: I ain't sayin' that! I ain't never tried to lose no game I ever played in.

GREY: Just don't say anything that would make Mr. Comiskey look bad. Say nothing about asking to be suspended or trying to show him the bribe money or writing him a letter during the off-season offering to tell all you knew.

JOE: If I don't then I won't go to jail? The gamblers won't come after Katie'n me? I'll be able to keep playin' ball?

GREY: We'll protect you, Joe. All we want to do is get the gamblers out of the game.

(JOE and GREY exit as two

FANS enter.)

FAN 1: Gone are the days when my heart was young and gay.

FAN 2: When my heart was young and gay.

FAN 1: Gone are my friends from those cotton mills far away.

FAN 2: I'm comin'!

FAN 1: I'm comin'!

FAN 2: For my head is bendin' low.

FAN 1: I hear those gentle voices.

BOTH: Callin' for Shoeless Joe.

(The FANS become REPORTERS

as GREY enters with JOE.)

REPORTER 1*:* Are you going to confess, Joe?

REPORTER 2: How much did you get, Jackson?

(Lightbulbs flash. JOE is staggered.)

GREY: It's Ok, Joe, I'm here…Come on, guys, leave him alone! Can't you see he's under a terrible strain?

REPORTER 1: How much money did you get, Joe?

REPORTER 2: Yeah, how much and where'd the dough come from?

(Lightbulbs flash.)

JOE: Get the hell away from me!

(JOE tries to get by, but is blocked

by REPORTER 2.)

REPORTER 2: Who else was involved?

REPORTER 1: Did you try to lose every game? Even those you won?

JOE: I wish I never heard of baseball! I never wanted to come up North. I knew somethin' terrible was gonna happen. You sons of bitches have been waitin' for somethin' like this to finish me off!

(The REPORTERS write feverishly

as JOE pushes past them.)

GREY: Take it easy, Joe, take it easy. Everything will be OK.

(GREY scowls at the

REPORTERS.)

GET OUTTA HERE!

ANNOUNCER: And now pitching for the State, Hartley Replogle!

(*Cheers are heard as Prosecutor REPLOGLE enters trotting. He waves at GREY and gives him the "OK" sign.*)

GREY: Did you see that, Joe? He really is on your side. He'll lay the questions right in there nice and easy. No curve balls, no shiners, no spitters. Now, go in there and hit a homer!

JOE: How can I get a hit offa him if I don't got no bat?

GREY: You don't need one. You're Shoeless Joe...an American hero.

(*REPLOGLE does an elaborate windup as he "pitches" the question.*)

REPLOGLE: Did anybody offer you any money to help throw the World Series?　　　　　　　199

JOE: Yes…Chick Gandil…He was the instigator of i[

(REPLOGLE looks in for th
sign. He smiles, shaking h
head "Yes.")

REPLOGLE: How much did Gandil promise you?

JOE: Twenty thousand dollars if I would take part. I g
paid 5,000.

REPLOGLE: And you said you would take part?

JOE: Yes, sir.

REPLOGLE: Who paid you the 5,000 dollars?

JOE: Lefty Williams brought it in my room and threw
down.

REPLOGLE: What did you say to Williams when
threw down the 5,000 dollars?   2[

JOE: I asked him what the hell'd come off here.

REPLOGLE: Weren't you in the inner circle?

JOE: No, I was never with them. It was mentioned to me in Boston. They asked me what would I consider, 10,000 dollars? And I said no. And when we returned to Chicago, he told me he would give me 20 and I said no again.

REPLOGLE: Did it ever occur to you to tell about this before this?

JOE: I offered to come here last fall. I would've come here last fall if they would've brought me in…I did tell them once. "I'm not gonna be in it." I'll just get outta that altogether.

REPLOGLE: Who did you say that to?

JOE: Chick Gandil.

REPLOGLE: What did he say?   201

JOE: He said I was in it already and I might as well stay in. I said, "I can go to the Boss and have every damn one of ya pulled out in the limelight." He said it wouldn't be well for me if I did that.

REPLOGLE: What did you say?

JOE: I told him any time they wanted to have me knocked off, to have me knocked off.

REPLOGLE: What did he say?

JOE: Just laughed.

REPLOGLE: Did you make any intentional errors during the World Series?

JOE: No, sir, not durin' the whole Series.

REPLOGLE: Did you bat to win?

JOE: Yes.   202

REPLOGLE: And run the bases to win?

JOE: Yes, sir.

REPLOGLE: And fielded the balls at the outfield to win?

JOE: I did.

REPLOGLE: Did you do anything to throw these games?

JOE: No, sir.

REPLOGLE: Any game in the Series?

JOE: Not a one. I didn't have an error or make no misplay...I tried to win all the time.

REPLOGLE: Weren't you much peeved that you only got 5,000 dollars and you expected to get 20?   203

JOE: No, I was ashamed of myself.

(REPLOGLE stops pitching as he

addresses the court.)

REPLOGLE: This is an unusual case as it deals with a class of men who are involved in our Great National Game, which all red-blooded American men follow. This game has been made the subject of a crime. The public, the press, the club owner and even the small boy playing on the sandlots have been swindled.

(REPLOGLE exits as JUDGE LANDIS enters.

LANDIS: No player who throws a game. No player who undertakes or promises to throw a game. No player who sits in a conference with a bunch of crooked players and gamblers where the ways and means of throwing a game are discussed and does not promptly tell his club about it, will ever play professional baseball ever again.

(LANDIS exits as the NEWSBOY enters.

NEWSBOY: PLLL-AAAY BA-iiiiLLL! EXTRA! EXTRA! READ ALL ABOUT IT! EIGHT WHITE SOX PLAYERS INDICTED! CICOTTE GOT TEN THOUSAND, JACKSON FIVE THOUSAND!

(The NEWSBOY pulls a piece of paper

from his pocket and reads.)

Newsboy resolution passed un...unan... unanimously! Resolved that the eight White Sox players be condemned and punished for their murderous blow at the kids' game. And that the honest White Sox players be commended for their manly stand against the Benedict Arnolds of baseball.

VOICES: TRAITORS!

(The NEWSBOY exits as GREY

pats JOE on the back.)

GREY: You did fine, Joe, just fine.

JOE: Did I? Maybe I shoulda told 'em 'bout the letter I wrote and how I asked to be benched before the Series started.

GREY: They never would've believed you, Joe.

REPORTER 1: How ya feel, Joe, after testifying?

JOE: Okay, I guess. Got some things offa my che:
Risberg threatened to bump me off if I squawked. Swe·
is a hard guy.

(SWEDE enters and glares at JOE

then exits. GREY and REPORTERS

exit as TY COBB enters.)

COBB: You shithead, Joe! How could ya be so stupi
Ya can't trust nobody. 'Specially Yankees. Ain't
learned that yet?

JOE: Whaddya talkin' about, Ty?

COBB: Ya shoulda been like me. Always on the atta·
That's what I done when Dutch Leonard accused me
bettin' on a game. Leonard knew I'd tear him a new o·
if he come to the hearin'.

2

JOE: But I cooperated. Cooperated jus' like they told me to so's I could keep playin' ball.

COBB: People love bringin' their heroes down, crashin' down if possible. You've fallen from grace, Joe. They'll make a symbol outta ya. A warnin' to others. Why, if it could happen to Shoeless Joe, an American Hero, it could happen to you.

JOE: Ain't I still Shoeless Joe, an American Hero? Harry Grey said I done good...Real good.

COBB: Ya shouldn't have let them do this to ya, Joe. They're gonna eat ya alive, boy.

(RING enters reading a newspaper.)

RING: "From out of the hills of South Carolina there came a raw-boned, strong, active youth...Some scout had discovered him up in the hills playing baseball. In a short time, he had risen from a poor mill boy to the rank of a player in the major leagues...Each season he and Ty Cobb battled for the honors of hitting and Shoeless Joe

RING: (*cont.*) Jackson, the unknown, rough, uncouth mill boy became one of the most famous men in the United States…He could not read nor write…There came a day when a crook spread money before this ignorant idol and he fell. For a few dollars, which perhaps seemed a fortune to him, he sold his honor. And when the inevitable came, Joe Jackson went before a body of men and told the story of his own infamy. While he related the sordid details to the stern-faced, shocked men, there gathered outside the big stone building a group of boys…

(BOY enters.)

They did not talk of baseball or anything else…After an hour, a man guarded like a felon by other men, emerged from the door. He did not swagger. He slunk along between his guardians, and the kids with wide eyes and tightening throats watched. And one, bolder than the others, pressed forward and said…

BOY: Say it ain't so, Joe.

RING: Jackson gulped back a sob. The shame of utter shame flushed his face.

JOE: I'm afraid it is, kid."

(The BOY runs off as RING

exits after him.)

JOE: That never happened.

COBB: It didn't? It sure does make great folklore. See ya 'round, Jackson.

(COBB exits as KATIE enters

and looks at JOE.)

JOE: It never happened. No kid come up to me after I testified. I walked out of that there courthouse with a bailiff, got in a car and drove off. Nobody said nuttin' to me.

KATIE: I know, sweetheart.

JOE: It ain't so.

KATIE: I know.   209

JOE: I ain't no myth. Never wanted to be one. I'm jus
a man.

KATIE: Y'er the man I love, Joey, and always will.

JOE: Don't care what people say 'bout me. All tha
matters is what the Man Upstairs thinks and He know
I'm innocent.

KATIE: And I know it, too.

JOE: It ain't so.

(KATIE embraces and rocks JOE.

KATIE: I know, Joey, I know.

JOE: It ain't so.

(CURTAIN)

AFTERWORD

During a 2018 White Sox broadcast, Jason Benetti asked Manager Rick Renteria, "What one person in baseball, dead or alive, would you want to meet?" After a brief pause Renteria replied, "Probably Mr. Jackson of the White Sox...Talk to him...See what actually happened back in the day." Surprised, the announcer exclaimed, "Shoeless Joe!!"

"Correct, Shoeless Joe," the skipper proudly responded.

"Really?! Why him of all people?" Jason asked.

"I believe him. I believe this guy went out to win," Renteria explained. Later in the broadcast, Benetti asked his partner, Cy Young Award winner Steve Stone, what he thought of the exchange.

"He hit what, .375?" Stone replied, "It doesn't seem to me that Joe Jackson tried to lose."

MALLEABLE STATS

What more could Joe Jackson have done to prove th
he had played to win throughout the 1919 World Serie
His awesome batting average--should that not have be
enough? He also set a record for the most hits in a Wor
Series (12) that lasted for decades; made no errors a
hit the only home run in the Series; scored five runs a
knocked in six on a team that scored just 20; led his tea
in slugging percentage; and advanced the most runne
on the team, 15, including Games One, Two and Fo
that the Sox lost. What more need be said?

More than any other sport, baseball relies on stats
separate the great and the near-great from the rest of t
pack. However, Joe's incredible record has not be
enough to satisfy everyone. Bill Lamb writes in l
article, "An Ever-Changing Story" featured in the Spri
2019 *SABR Baseball Research Journal*:

> "Statistics are always malleable, subject to
> partisan manipulation. More rigorous
> examination of how the 1919 World Series
> unfolded…yields a damning assessment of Joe
> performance. During the first five games, the
> outer limit of the fix duration in most minds,
> clean-up batter Jackson notably underproduce
> failing to drive in a single White Sox run. Mo
> of Jackson's gaudy stats were compiled only
> after the fix had been abandoned and the Blach
> Sox had begun trying to win."[1]   2

Lamb argues Joe hit a "soft" .316, 6-for-19, in the first five games because he had no RBIs. He went 5-for-7 in Games 2 and 3 a robust, but apparently "soft" .714 against a Reds pitching staff considered by many to be the best in the Senior Circuit. They were so good that Christy Mathewson felt they had a real chance to win the Series. While Jackson did not drive in any runs during the first five games, he did score two of the White Sox six runs including what proved to be the winning run in Game 3. If Game 4 is added, Joe hit .545 during a three-game stretch of the five games. While Lamb also writes Joe was "hardly without accomplices in underachievement,"[2] he neglects to mention the stats of the honest Sox, Eddie and Shano Collins, Ray Schalk, Nemo Leibold, Eddie Murphy and Byrd Lynn, who hit a combined .130 (7-for-54) with just one RBI in those first five games.

Tim Hornbaker writes in his Jackson biography that Joe "failed to produce a total of eight times when men were on base, seven of them with runners in scoring position."[3] However, applying a "more rigorous examination" yields a positive assessment of Joe's performance. He did produce five times in the Series with runners in scoring position going 5-for-14 for an excellent .357 batting average. Jackson went 6-for-17 hitting .353 with runners on which is consistent with his career .356 average. Runners also moved up three of the times that he failed to get a hit.

In the 1917 World Series, which was won by the White Sox, Jackson hit an even "softer" .304 driving in two compared to the six RBIs he had in 1919. He had no hits in three of the six games. He had no extra-base hits in '17; four in '19. Curiously, Joe also went 6-for-19 in the first five games of the '17 Series, but did drive in a pair in Game 2. He failed to get a hit 11 times with runners on base hitting just .214 with runners on in the Series. Noting the "randomness of baseball," Grantland Rice wrote, "on certain days, a superstar lived up to the expectations of audiences, while on others he might prove powerless at the plate...the unpredictability of the national game."[4]

RIGOROUS EXAMINATION

Regarding his performance in the 1919 World Series, Joe's teammate Eddie Murphy said, "Jackson's hitting was wonderful...He was robbed of a number of hits by sensational fielding, but even so he came through with many a timely clout."[5] In Game Four, which was a White Sox loss, Joe hit a rocket to second baseman Morrie Rath, who, like many infielders, had great difficulty handling one of Joe's trademark "blue darters." The smash was initially ruled a hit, but later changed to an error. In today's game, such hard-hit balls are frequently scored as hits. If the initial ruling had stood, Joe would have hit .368 in the first five games and .406 overall for the Series! Would that have been enough to convert Joe's critics?

In addition to Murphy, other teammates praised Joe's performance. Eddie Collins said, "Jackson maintained his reputation with the stick,"[6] and throughout the years he played with Joe, "he did everything right."[7] Ray Schalk said that "Joe Jackson hit as hard as he did during the season, or even a little better."[8] Shano Collins, however, disagreed, saying of Joe and others, "very few of these hits were made at the proper time and that errors were made when they cost the most."[9] Joe, however, made no errors and, as noted above, hit .353 with runners on base. And how did Shano himself hit at "the proper time" with runners on? He went 0-for-4!

Oscar Reichow of the *Chicago Daily News* reported "Jackson certainly demonstrated that a World's Series makes little difference to him. He played up to his standard."[10] Former Major Leaguer Fred Luderus testified "Jackson had compiled 'a wonderful batting average'…against a Reds pitching staff that had been 'the strongest in baseball'."[11] The American Statistician reported that "Almost every statistical view of the game data supports the contention that Joe Jackson played to his full potential in the 1919 World Series."[12] I would imagine their examination was quite rigorous. 215

Gene Carney wrote that Comiskey's "grandson has sworn for the record that the Comiskey family's belief was that Jackson neither conspired to throw nor attempted to throw any or all games in the 1919 World Series."[13] Lamb writes that Comiskey himself testified he had "observed nothing dishonest in Jackson's Series play" and the slugger had "played good ball...Nor did Comiskey suspect Jackson of crooked play at any other time during his six-season tenure with the club."[14] He did, however, question Joe's "too shallow positioning on a Game One drive to left field that went over Jackson's head."[15] David Fleitz in his Jackson biography, while acknowledging Joe played errorless ball, notes three triples were hit to Joe's left field position, including two by pitchers. Most triples are hit to right or center field. However, William Herzog II points out outfielders in the dead-ball era played much shallower than they do today.[17] Team captain Eddie Collins, who has been described as the greatest field general ever, was in charge of positioning Joe and the other fielders and he said Joe did "everything right."

IT AIN'T SO, IS IT, LEFTY?

Joe's detractors believe, despite his stats, he must have been involved in the fix because he attended meetings with the crooked players and gamblers; he "accepted" $5,000 from his pal Lefty Williams; he didn't report what was happening to team management; and he confessed to the grand jury. According to Lamb, Eddie Cicotte testified "the World Series fix was first discussed at a players meeting conducted at the Ansonia Hotel in New York around September 10 or 12, 1919"[18] and Jackson was present. However, as Herzog has pointed out, the meeting must have taken place on September 16 or 17 when the team was in New York City. In fact, they were in Washington on September 10 and Philadelphia on the 12th. Joe could not have been present since "Gandil had not even approached Jackson about participating in the fix and would not do so for another day or two"[19] when they were in Boston on September 19-20.

Joe was not at the Ansonia Hotel meeting. *Drunk History* got that wrong, too. Neither was he present at the meetings held at the Warner Hotel in Chicago nor the Sinton Hotel in Cincinnati. Gamblers Sleepy Bill Burns and Billy Maharg confirmed Joe was not at the meetings they attended and Maharg said he had no contact with him at any time. Burns said in his deposition that Lefty Williams informed Black Sox ringleader Chick Gandil that he "was kind of representing Jackson for fix purposes."[20]

Lamb writes:

"For Jackson's grand jury testimony about his f
involvement to be some sort of implant
fabrication one must also conclude that eve
other Black Sox who named Jackson as a f
participant—Eddie Cicotte, Lefty Willian
inferentially Happy Felsch, even Chick Gan
—maliciously accused an innocent man. N
reason why his teammates would implica
Jackson falsely has ever been advanced becau
there is none."[21]

I believe, however, the Black Sox implicated Jacks
precisely because Lefty falsely told Gandil, who to
Cicotte and Felsch and anyone else, that Williams w
"kind of" representing Joe. It was Lefty's perfidy th
did Joe in. Why did he betray his friend? Obviously,
an attempt to get more money from the gamblers w
wanted assurances that the team's best hitter was part
the plot.

In his book *Black Sox in the Courtroom,* Lamb writ
Lefty's deposition in Joe's 1924 civil suit was "repl
with recitals of conversations, cash payments, and oth
fix-connected events implicating Jackson in the Seri
conspiracy."[22] When cross-examined, however, by Joe
attorney, Raymond Cannon, Williams admitted he lie

> CANNON: Did Joe Jackson tell you at any tin
> prior to or during the World Series that you
> could use his name in dealing with the gambler

WILLIAMS: No, sir.   2

CANNON: In reference to throwing the games?

WILLIAMS: No, sir.

CANNON: Did you have any talk with him in that connection at all?

WILLIAMS: No, sir.

CANNON: At any time?

WILLIAMS: No, sir.

CANNON: To your knowledge did Joe Jackson know his name was being used by anybody for the purpose of dealing with the gamblers?

WILLIAMS: No, sir.[23]

"It ain't so, is it, Lefty?" How appropriate that would have been if it had been said by the "kid in knee pants" who "dodged between the bailiffs and grabbed him by the arm. 'It ain't so, is it, Lefty?' he cried in terms that demanded a negative answer. Williams didn't answer and the kid slunk back, a dazed look on his freckled face." [24]

Williams might have rationalized his treachery by thinking he was looking out for Joe because the star's name had been used so Jackson had, in effect, earned the money. David Fleitz argues Gandil would not have given Joe $5,000 if he had felt Jackson was playing to win. He didn't give Weaver any money.[25] Perhaps, Gandil agreed with Lefty that Joe deserved the money for "allowing" them to use his name no matter how he performed in the Series. Perhaps, he hoped if Lefty could get his friend to "accept" the money, he then would be a part of the plot and would keep his mouth shut. How stunned Lefty must have been when he tried to give his pal the bribe and Joe refused to "accept" it! Jackson, who didn't know his name was being used, argued with the southpaw telling him that he was going to inform Comiskey. Lefty, in exasperation, threw the envelope down. How stunned Joe must have been when team secretary Harry Grabiner, who "could be a pit bull when necessary, and with Comiskey behind him, he had the confidence to resort to hardball tactics with players if need be,"[26] slammed the door in the star's face when Joe asked to speak with the club owner about the Series and shouted at him to go away. To whom could Joe turn? The reporters all seemed to be Comiskey's comrades. As Hornbaker writes, "A great percentage of writers were fully on the side of the owners, and one could only guess whether kickbacks or friendships gave way to such interests."[27] Also, Joe must have been concerned about his and his wife's safety. If Gandil and Risberg heard he was squawking to Manager Gleason, his life could be in danger. And everyone knew what the gamblers could do.

LYRIA

Lamb asserts "in most minds" that the fix was over after the first five games. I find that difficult to believe. The Sox were down four games to one in the best-of-nine Series. Perhaps they tried to win Game Six because of the gamblers' double-cross. They also won Game Seven, but the plan had always been to get Cicotte a win to help him with his contract negotiations.

Jacob Pomrenke, Chairman of the Black Sox Scandal Research Committee, indicated he does not believe an anecdote that appeared in an article in *The New Yorker* in 1959 about a threat made against Lefty Williams prior to Game Eight. Pomrenke stated:

> "There is exactly one piece of evidence that Lefty Williams was threatened…A first person essay…This story came from someone who was a neighbor of the Williamses in Chicago in the 1930s two decades earlier. He was a little boy about six or seven years old at this time, and twenty years later he grows up and he's writing an essay for *The New Yorker* the week or two after Lefty Williams had died. He claims that he was a neighbor boy in the same apartment house in Chicago, and he had gone over to the Williamses house and he was sitting in Lefty Williams' kitchen with his wife, Lyria…This is the first time that this little boy is discovering

that the World Series had been fixed and that hi
neighbor had been part of it, and he claims that
Lyria told him that Lefty had been threatened.
And that's the only source for the myth that
Lefty Williams got threatened in Game Eight
other than Billy Maharg later on when he was
clearly no longer involved, had mentioned it
once too … That's it. That's the only source for
the idea that Lefty Williams was threatened. So
the evidence is extremely thin and it's based on
an anecdote told forty years later by someone
who was six years old at the time, remembering
something that was said in Lefty Williams'
kitchen in Chicago…So there's really no real
credible evidence that Lefty Williams was ever
threatened and, in fact, there's a lot more
evidence that the fix was off by this time."[28]

I find the article, "Requiem for a Southpaw", to b
very credible.   It was written by J.M. Flagler,
distinguished journalist, who wrote scores of articles fo
The New Yorker.   He was Lefty and Lyria's neighbo
in the early 1930s.   He was not "six years old at th
time" since, according to his obituary, he was born i
either 1921 or 22.   He was, therefore, very likel
between the ages of nine and 13 when he had hi
conversation with Lyria.   He describes himself in hi
article as being "in the eight-to-fourteen set"[29] when h
was their neighbor.

Flagler also wrote for *The New York Times Magazine, The Saturday Review, The New Republic, Look* and other publications. He taught a course in magazine writing at the prestigious Columbia Graduate School of Journalism and wrote for major TV programs. He was also a World War II veteran who survived the bloody, brutal battle of Okinawa.[30] Lyria must have been aware of the 1959 article. She lived until 1975. I have never read she ever disputed anything that she was attributed to have said in the piece.

According to Lamb, Billy Maharg, a major figure in the scandal's unfolding, "heard that Attell and Midwestern gamblers had revived the fix, intimidating Sox starter Lefty Williams into his dreadful Game 8 performance."[31] Hugh Fullerton was told by gamblers that the game would be over early. It would be the "biggest first inning you ever saw."[32] In fact, Williams got knocked out in the first.

What would have happened to the Black Sox if they had won Games Eight and Nine and gone on to win the 1919 World Series? Can there be any doubt that they would have put their lives and those of their families at risk? One writer opined that Lefty Williams "would have been shot while on the mound."[33] Gangster Frank Costello, when asked what would have happened if Joe had talked, responded "Jackson wouldn't have made it home."[34]

I think one of the reasons Joe's critics don't want believe Game Eight was fixed is because they th would have to explain how a crooked Jackson went for-5 in the game with three RBIs and a homer. He reported to have barely missed a second home run in t game when he flied out to deep center field. How wou they have explained that? If only that ball had flown ov the fence, giving Joe two round-trippers in the Seri And if only Joe's smash in Game Four had not be changed from a hit to an error, he would have gotten hits in the Series, a record that would still stand tod 100 years later, and he would have had a batting avera of .438! How could anyone then say he was trying lose? If only...

LETTERS

Joe's critics cannot deny that, in response to a let dated November 11, 1919 from Comiskey that stated:

> "There has been a great deal of adverse talk in
> which your name has been mentioned...
> reflecting on your integrity in the recent World
> Series...Would gladly pay your expenses to
> Chicago...if you wish to come on in reference
> the matter pertaining to the talk emanating from
> the World's Series,"[35]

Joe, via his wife, wrote back on November 15, 1919.
that letter, he indicated his surprise: 2

"to hear that my name has been connected with any scandle (sic) in the recent World Saires (sic) as I think my playing proved that I did all I could to win…I will be onley (sic) to (sic) glad to come to Chicago…and clear my name and whoever started this will have to prove his statements…I am sure I did all I could to win and I think my Record for the Series Will Show if you Look at it…And let me hear from you as to when you want me to come to Chicago."[36]

Unsurprisingly, Comiskey never responded.

TELL 'EM I WAS DRUNK

One of the most significant passages to me in Joe's 1920 grand jury testimony is his description of his encounter with gambler Sleepy Bill Burns in the lobby of the Sinton Hotel "the day the World's Series started." Joe testified Burns "told me about this stuff and I didn't know so much. I hadn't been around and I didn't know so much. (Burns) said, 'Where is Chick?' I said, 'I don't know.' He walked away from me." Clearly, going to look for Gandil who had apparently assured Burns that Joe was in on the plot. "I didn't know enough to talk to him about what they were going to plan or what they had planned. I wouldn't know it if I had (not?) seen him,"[37] Joe testified.

225

As Gene Carney writes, "Jackson told the grand jury in 1920 that he knew for sure that something fishy was going on when he was approached by a gambler the morning of Game One...(Burns) thought Jackson knew all about the fix, and left him quickly when he realized that he did not...(Joe) knew the gamblers thought he was in on the fix."[38] Herzog writes, "So, on the morning of October 1, 1919, Jackson knew the series was rigged. What did he do? The very thing he was condemned for not doing. He went to Kid Gleason and/or Charles Comiskey and notified the ball club."[39]

In Joe's 1949 *Sport Magazine* interview he stated, "I went to Mr. Charles Comiskey's room (at the Sinton Hotel) the night before the Series started and asked him to keep me out of the line-up...He refused, and I begged him, 'Tell the newspapers you just suspended me for being drunk, or anything, but leave me out of the Series and then there can be no question.' Hugh Fullerton was in the room and heard the whole thing. He offered to testify for me at my trial later, and he came all the way out to Chicago to do it."[40] The interview was conducted 30 years after the event and Joe was an elderly man, which accounts, I believe, for his mistakenly saying the meeting took place the night before the Series and not the following morning. Lamb writes of:

"The stunning allegation that Jackson was so troubled by World Series fix rumors swirling about that he went to club owner Comiskey's hotel room in Cincinnati the night before Game One and pleaded to be removed from the line-up, lest his reputation be besmirched by playing in a rigged championship match. And this, Jackson said, was all witnessed by syndicated sports columnist Hugh Fullerton 'who offered to testify for me at my trial later.' In fact, neither Fullerton nor any other witness was summoned to the stand by the Jackson defense. Three years later, however, Fullerton did testify as a White Sox defense witness in the Jackson civil suit."

Where he apparently testified falsely. More on that later.

Lamb continues:

"More important, Fullerton's testimony contains no mention of Jackson trying to beg off playing in the 1919 Series. Nor does the alleged event appear anywhere in Fullerton's writings on the scandal, inexplicable given that star player Jackson begging Comiskey to keep him out of the World Series would have been a sensational story that any sportswriter would have rushed into newsprint—had it ever happened."[41]

Fullerton did write an article for *The Sporting News* in 1935, four years after Comiskey's death, entitled " Recall" in which he describes his own encounters with gamblers, including Burns, the day before the Series began tipping him off that the fix was in. The following morning, he "talked with two big-shot Chicago gamblers, who told me flat-footedly that the Series was fixed for Cincinnati to win." Fullerton continues, "I was much upset and went to Comiskey to urge him to take some action."[42]

Pomrenke writes regarding a Comiskey interview with Sid Keener published in December 13, 1930 in which the owner admitted "the first inkling I received that something was crooked came when I was informed several hours before Game One…While I was holding conference in my (Sinton) Hotel room." Pomrenke states that the interview does "lend some credence to Hugh Fullerton's claim that the White Sox owner had knowledge about the fix before a single pitch was thrown."[43] It also lends credence, I believe, to Jackson' story that he spoke to Comiskey in his Sinton Hotel room, which I also believe to be the morning of Game One, after his encounter with the gambler Burns. How else would Joe have known Fullerton was meeting with Comiskey at that time?

FULLERTON RECALLS

Hugh Fullerton concludes his 1935 article writing, "But today, more than 15 years later, the full story never has been told and never will be, because Johnson, Comiskey, Herrmann and Alf Austrian, the only ones who knew it all, are dead."[44] And now, 100 years after the scandal, Fullerton, Jackson and all the other participants are gone. So, we are never going to know exactly what happened.

I believe Joe when he said Fullerton was prepared to testify for him and travelled to Chicago to attend the 1921 trial. So why did the Defense call no witnesses and rest their case? Lamb writes, "Little public explanation was provided for this unanticipated change in defense strategy. All that could be gotten from counsel was the comment that it was not necessary to put the players on the witness stand because the 'state has made no case'."[45] Perhaps the Defense didn't trust Fullerton, who was known to be a comrade of Comiskey, the owner who lavished "attention—via personal access, sumptuous post-game buffets, and a well-stocked liquor cabinet-- upon Chicago sports scribes, most of whom revered Comiskey."[46] He may have been suspected of being on Comiskey's payroll working for what *Collyer's Eye* described as "the suppression bureau."[47] Although he may well have assured Joe that he would be willing to testify on his behalf, it's hard to believe Fullerton would have said anything that would have put Comiskey in a bad light.   229

Herzog maintains Fullerton had a "long-standin animosity towards Jackson."[48] In 1911, Joe's first fι season in the Majors, Fullerton wrote, "A man who caι read or write…simply can't expect to meet t requirements of big league baseball as it is play today."[49] In his most famous article that contained t phrase, "It ain't true, Joe, is it?", written when t scandal broke, Hugh refers to the illiterate Joe as "t ignorant idol," as if what happened was predictable frc the beginning. Fullerton always fancied himself brilliant prognosticator having predicted the "Hitle Wonders" White Sox would defeat the mighty Cubs the 1906 World Series.

Why didn't Fullerton ever write anything about Joc request to be suspended? It can also be asked why it to the reporter 16 years to write about his own warni about a fix to Comiskey on the morning of Game Oι That, too, "would have been a sensational story that a sportswriter would have rushed into newsprint." Hu chose not to write about his concerns until four yeέ after the owner's death. At the end of the 1935 artic he states "when the Series finally ended, I feared r branding of the game as a fix might lose my friendsh with Charles Comiskey." He did not lose his friendsh but he very likely would have had he reported Joc appeal to be suspended "before the first pitch had be thrown in the 1919 World Series" while his friend w still alive.   2

If Fullerton had reported Joe's request after the owner's death, he would have had to explain why he wrote his "It ain't true, Joe, is it?" piece, which implicated the ballplayer and is widely considered to have been apocryphal by Joe's defenders and detractors alike, without mentioning Joe's begging to be removed from the line-up before the start of the 1919 World Series.

A NEVER-CHANGING STORY

Lamb writes, "When it came to his involvement in the corruption of the 1919 World Series, Shoeless Joe Jackson rarely told the same story twice."[50] Joe did, however, from his 1920 grand jury testimony to his dying day consistently state he always played to win. He even said of all his accomplishments, his performance in the 1919 World Series was the one of which he was most proud.

Lamb refers several times to "an extended post-grand jury interview"[51] that Jackson allegedly gave to "the gathered pressmen"[52] where the slugger reveals "that attempts to dump Game Three had been frustrated by Dickey Kerr's shutout pitching,"[53] admitting "the eight of us did our best to kick it."[54] Jacob Pomrenke stated "Joe Jackson claimed that they were trying to lose Game Three. He told reporters (plural) that they were trying to lose the game that Dickey Kerr won because he wasn't part of the plot."[55]

It is also alleged Joe decided to confess because he was upset about being brushed off by Gandil, who had retired after the 1919 World Series and whom Jackson had not seen for a year, Risberg and McMullin when he complained about being short-changed $15,000 in bribe money. "This next-day reportage, ignored by Jackson supporters and mostly neglected by scandal chroniclers, has never been discredited,"[56] Lamb declares. This has been "ignored and neglected" for good reason simply because it is not credible. That Joe, who just hours after emphatically testifying before the grand jury that he had always played to win and who, throughout the remainder of his life, repeated that sentiment, would say he tried to "kick" Game Three or he decided to confess because he didn't receive all of his promised bribe money, is not believable. Joe was specifically asked about Game Three by Assistant State Attorney Hartley Replogle during his testimony:

> REPLOGLE: In the third game Kerr pitched there, 1 to nothing. Did you see anything there that would lead you to believe anyone was trying to throw the game?
>
> JOE: No, sir. I think if you would look that record up, I drove in two and hit one.[57]

Actually, Joe went 2-for-3 in the game, made no errors, did not drive in any runs, but did score what proved to be the winning run, which was hardly the performance of a ballplayer who was trying to "kick" the game. The score of Game Three was actually 3-0 and not 1-0. There is nothing in the article indicating Joe gave an interview to "the gathered pressmen." Lamb notes the article was "Initially printed in the *Chicago Tribune*, September 29, 1920, and then circulated nationwide via the AP wire service. See, e.g., *Steubenville* (Ohio) *Herald-Star*, September 29, 1920."[58]

As Charles Fountain writes, "It is beyond dispute that most newspaper exclusives in those days were scoops mainly because they were made up."[59] It is my belief, therefore, the interview was made up by the *Chicago Tribune* reporter who wrote the article which was picked up by other newspapers via the AP wire. There is no proof of any such gathering of pressmen. The newspapers were rife with phony quotes allegedly from Jackson's grand jury testimony that he had just tapped at the ball; deliberately struck out with men in scoring position; and moved slowly to balls hit to him. He said none of those things during his testimony. According to Carney, newspapers didn't print Joe's quotes that he had played to win. Instead, they "fabricated quotes."[60]

Lamb, too, has written Jackson was "victimized by specious accounts of his testimony."[61] And Herzog has observed newspapers published "specious excerpts as though they were Jackson's own words when, in fact, they were manufactured by the papers themselves."[62] As noted above, Hugh Fullerton's famous "It ain't true, Joe, is it?" article is widely considered to be false by Joe's defenders and detractors alike. Yet, Lamb refers to the alleged interview often as proof of Joe's culpability, while never once mentioning in "An Ever-Changing Story" the vitally important exchange of letters between Joe and Comiskey in November of 1919.

ALF AND THE TWO JOES

The most damaging problem that Joe's detractors face is explaining how a player who set a batting record could possibly have been throwing the World Series. Lamb disparages Joe's achievement arguing that he hit a "soft" .316 during the first five games of the Series. He declares a "more rigorous examination of Joe's performance yields a damning assessment."

Joe's supporters, meanwhile, must explain why there seemed to be two Joes testifying before the grand jury. One Joe said he always played to win while the other claimed to be a part of the nefarious plot. The key to understanding the contradiction lies in the major role played by Alf (as Fullerton referred to him) Austrian who was both the attorney for the White Sox and Comiskey's personal lawyer.

A reader of Lamb's article could be excused for believing that Austrian, variously described as "not a baseball fan"[63] who had never met Joe and had "rarely, if ever, attended a ballgame,"[64] was "out-of-the-loop" and what he was learning when the scandal broke was primarily new to him. Lamb writes:

> "When Joe Jackson was first confronted about his fix involvement in the Austrian law office, his inquisitors had only limited information about the matter…Comiskey…had presumably imparted the intelligence uncovered by his operatives to Austrian…The only specific intel that Comiskey had about the fix that implicated …Jackson…was the hearsay supplied to him by disgruntled St. Louis gamblers Harry Redmon and Joe Pesch. And that intel lacked detail. Sox attorney Austrian knew even less."[65]

In his book *Black Sox in the Courtroom*, howeve[r]
Lamb describes the meeting with Redmon and Pes[e]
"where they repeated what they knew to club own[er]
Comiskey and various club officials. As Redm[on]
recalled, Sox lawyer Alfred Austrian did most of t[he]
talking on the other side."[66] How could Austrian kn[ow]
"even less" when he attended the meeting with the cl[ub]
officials and the gamblers where he "did most of t[he]
talking"?

Lamb has written:

> "The extent to which Comiskey's post-Seri[es]
> conduct was influenced by club counsel Austri[an]
> is unknowable, but Comiskey biographer T[im]
> Hornbaker asserts that the Old Roman…l[eft]
> management of the simmering scandal mostly [in]
> the hands of Austrian and Grabiner. A[n]
> increased Austrian involvement in club affairs [is]
> undeniable, embodied in his designation as
> Chicago White Sox vice president…in cl[ub]
> reports filed in early 1920."[67]

Charles Fountain writes Comiskey met with Austrian:

> "less than a week after the Series end[ed]
> Comiskey brought Austrian up to date on w[hat]
> he knew, what he suspected, and what he fear[ed]
> …As the Black Sox story unfolded…nothi[ng]
> happened beyond Austrian's awareness. And

2

much of what happened during that time happened because Austrian and his client wanted it to. The nearly year-long cover-up; the confessions of Eddie Cicotte, Joe Jackson and Lefty Williams...all bear Austrian's mark...He was a virtuoso in closed-door negotiation and deal making...Comiskey...was interested in three things ...preserving his business, preserving his reputation, and preserving his championship baseball team...If the whole sordid story (of the scandal) was to come out, it had to seem as though Comiskey was the principal cleanser. Austrian first launched a plan for a reward offer. As he did for many of the statements Comiskey made during the unfolding of the scandal, Austrian had a hand in writing it...The ($20,000) reward offer was genius...It insured that any gambler (or) ballplayer...with information real or imagined would now be bringing that information to the White Sox...(which) would become the repository for all things scandal, and the information thus gathered could be evaluated and used in ways that would best serve Charles A. Comiskey: burying it if they could; revealing it only if (they) had to; and judging the bulk of it to be "not credible" and thus not deserving of the reward."[68]

Can there be any doubt, also, that Alf was completely aware of the exchange of letters between Joe and Comiskey in November of 1919? Can there be any doubt that Austrian played a role in Comiskey's decision not to respond to Joe's offer to return to Chicago to clear his name and tell all that he knew? It is clear to me that Austrian and Comiskey did not want to hear what Joe had to say. If they had heard Jackson out, Austrian would have had all the information that he would need when he met with the baseball great in his office in September of 1920. Lamb declares "nothing in the canons of professional ethics conferred upon Austrian any duty to individual White Sox players. His professional obligation was to safeguard the best interests of his client: Charles Comiskey, and his corporate alter ego, the White Sox corporation."[69] The players, however, did not know this.

FALSE CONFESSIONS

When Shoeless Joe met with Austrian, he must have been frightened, confused and, if not intoxicated, severely hung over after a night of heavy drinking. He was a man who has been described as relying too much on others for guidance. Teammate Shano Collins said the slugger was "easily influenced."[70] Fullerton

238

described Joe as "'something of a boy himself,' clearly referring to his purity in mind and vulnerability."[71] Herzog asserts that "It is no insult to Joe Jackson's intelligence to say that he was no match for Alfred Austrian."[72]

Lamb writes:

> "Jackson's account of the World Series fix was specific regarding events that he was involved in, full of peculiar detail, and highly incriminating, his claim of actually trying his best on the field notwithstanding…Jackson defenders confronting the issue usually try to explain away Shoeless Joe's grand jury testimony by describing it as no more than regurgitation of information supplied to him by his interrogators. And, regrettably, false confessions are a phenomenon that the criminal justice system has to deal with on a far-too-frequent basis. The Jackson grand jury testimony, however, betrays none of the indicia of a false confession. Here is why. The essential component of the false confession is knowledge of the details of the underlying offense by those questioning a suspect—for if the questioner does not know what happened, how can he implant such information in the mind of someone else? When Joe Jackson was

first confronted about his fix involvement in the Austrian law office, his inquisitors had only limited information about the matter."[73]

He is apparently referring to the Cicotte "Admissions" discussed below.

Lamb continues:

> "(Cicotte) supplied Austrian…with none of the fix-specific detail…about the hold up of fix payoffs blamed on Abe Attell; about the $5000 delivered to (Joe's) hotel room by Lefty Williams prior to Game Five…that Jackson would reveal to the grand jury…In short, Jackson's detail-specific grand jury testimony could not have been implanted in his mind by Austrian or (ASA) Replogle, because neither they nor Comiskey were aware of such details at the time."[74]

As indicated above, I believe Alf, who was "the repository of all things scandal", knew considerably more details than indicated by Lamb. He knew about Attell's double-cross since it was on the front page of newspapers across America in the gambler Billy Maharg interview on the very day Austrian met with Joe. Lamb has written that:

"Concrete evidence of 1919 World Series corruption was sparse. That abruptly changed, however, when fix insider Billy Maharg went public with claims that grand-jury targets like Eddie Cicotte, Joe Jackson and Lefty Williams had dumped Games One, Two and Eight in return for a gambler's payoff."[75]

However, Maharg did not "claim" Joe had dumped the games. Only Eddie Cicotte was named in the article.[76]

Austrian very likely knew about Lefty's offering Joe the bribe money if one believes, as I do, team secretary Harry Grabiner told Joe in February of 1920, when he signed him to a three-year contract, that they were aware Williams had offered him $5,000 and Joe still had the money. Austrian, therefore, could have implanted information in Joe's mind.

Other specific details that were not "implanted" by Alf were, I believe, readily imparted to him by the ballplayer:

1) Joe asked to be suspended from the Series prior to Game One. It is my belief, as a result of the coaching of Austrian whose main objective was to protect Comiskey, Joe did not mention this during his grand jury testimony.

2) He was approached by Gandil in Boston and offered $10,000 to participate in the plot which Joe refused.

3) Joe was approached by Chick in Chicago who increased the offer to $20,000. He again refused. Joe testified about both of these bribe offers and his refusals, but I believe Jackson also testified he agreed to take part as the result of Austrian coaching.

4) When Lefty came to his hotel room offering him the $5,000 bribe, Joe angrily refused after being told by Williams that his name had been used without his permission and he told the southpaw that he was going to inform Comiskey. Williams threw down the envelope containing the bribe in exasperation. Joe testified before the grand jury that Lefty threw the money down and they argued but did not mention he intended to tell Comiskey, I believe again, as the result of Austrian convincing Joe not to implicate the club owner.

5) Joe took the money to show the owner, but had the door slammed in his face by Grabiner who told him to go away. Joe testified he went to

Comiskey's office on October 10, 1919, but I am convinced was persuaded by Alf not to mention the details about being rebuffed to protect Comiskey.

6) Joe was told by Grabiner to keep the bribe money when he tricked Jackson into signing a three-year contract containing the 10-Day Clause in February 1920. I am confident that if Grabiner knew about the bribe, Austrian and Comiskey also must have known.

7) Joe received a letter dated November 11, 1919 from Comiskey offering to pay his expenses if he wished to return to Chicago to tell what he knew.

8) Joe immediately replied on November 15, 1919 informing the owner that he wanted to come and clear his name. Comiskey never responded. Jackson told the grand jury that he "offered to come here last fall in the investigation. I would have told it last fall if they would have brought me in."[77] He did not mention the letters, in my opinion, as the result of Austrian's coaching.

These details, these facts, these truths would have "exonerated Jackson—condemned Comiskey."[78] It's what Austrian did with these details along with the implanted information, as indicated above, that led to Joe making a false confession.

CICOTTE ADMISSIONS

According to Lamb, "After being confronted privately with Cicotte's admissions in the Austrian law office, Jackson telephoned the chambers of Judge McDonald. At first, Jackson maintained his innocence to an openly skeptical McDonald."[79] Fleitz reports Joe declared he was an honest man to which the Judge replied, "I know, Jackson, that you are not!"[80]

What exactly did Judge McDonald know when, as Lamb maintains, the specific details were so limited? Apparently, his statement was based on the Cicotte "Admissions." Lamb writes:

> "Nor had Eddie Cicotte been over-enlightening. Summoned to the Austrian office ahead of Jackson, a distraught Cicotte readily admitted his own complicity in the plot to fix the Series outcome. And he specifically named Joe Jackson as 'one of the men who were in on the deal'."[81]

The statement that Joe was "in on the deal", I am convincingly persuaded, was based on Lefty Williams' false claim that he was "kind of" representing Joe. Continuing, Lamb states, "But, otherwise, Cicotte had not been particularly forthcoming."[82] Cicotte may also have said Joe was present at the Ansonia Hotel meeting in New York City which was untrue because Joe had not yet been approached by Gandil soliciting his participation in the plot. So, McDonald's assertion that Joe was not honest appears to have been based on two erroneous or false Cicotte "Admissions."

THE SECOND PHONE CALL

A false confession is a result of "techniques used during interrogations...designed to break people down into a sense of complete despair before offering them one route out: a confession."[83] Joe, very likely under greater stress than he had ever known in his life, later said, "All I wanted to do was tell my story and get out."[84] Charles Fountain writes:

> "(Joe) was shrewd enough to tell Alfred
> Austrian that he wanted a lawyer of his own.
> (Cicotte and Williams made no such request.)
> Austrian had no obligation beyond human
> decency to help Joe Jackson get a lawyer; and
> he felt no compunction about putting the

> interests of his client (Comiskey) ahead of the civil rights of Joe Jackson. 'We can do you more good than a lawyer,' Jackson remembered Austrian telling him, saying he was working together with state's attorney Replogle and Judge McDonald, and if Jackson told them what he knew, they would take care of him and let him go home. "[85]

Is there really "nothing in the canon of professional ethics" to prevent something like this? How different Joe's fate would have been if he had had an attorney of his own who would have told him to testify to his truth and had his best interests in mind instead of those of Comiskey. Alf had to convince the ballplayer that his truths would not be believed. Austrian kept no notes during their three-hour meeting as he had when he met with Cicotte and Williams. He had no fear of them. He did fear as Comiskey feared, Jackson, who could expose the cover-up, providing AL president Ban Johnson with all the information that he would need to bring his mortal enemy, Comiskey, down.

Bill Veeck asserts "To a man like Austrian, there is no right or wrong. There are only tactics, stratagems, techniques--and results."[86] Exactly what techniques, what stratagems Austrian used to coach Joe into making a false confession, we will never know. All that mattered to the attorney were the results. It is my belief that in order to achieve his primary objective of protecting Comiskey, Austrian had to convince Joe that he must not implicate the club owner because Jackson needed his protection to stay out of jail and to avoid the wrath of the violent gamblers who might put Joe's family at risk if they thought he had double-crossed them.

I can imagine what Austrian, a "virtuoso of closed-door negotiations," may have said to Joe, who told Austrian that he only wanted to tell the truth: *The truth will not be believed. The Judge didn't believe you, Joe, nor will any jury. Cicotte named you. Say you were a part of the plot, Joe. Show remorse. Say you are ashamed of yourself. The dangerous gamblers, who can make a person disappear, will be furious if they find out you took their money, but were not in on the fix. Your wife, Katie, could be at risk as well. We will take care of both of you, Joe. Mr. Comiskey and I will protect you. We do not want either of you to get hurt. We are your friends. We like you. But you must not say anything that would make Mr. Comiskey look bad. If you do, we won't be able to protect you and Katie. We only want to get the gamblers out of the game.*

Joe may well have continued to resist until h "friend" Alf reminded him that he had kept the bri money. He had put it in the bank. It wouldn't matt that the only withdrawals were made to help his si sister. *You could go to jail, Joe.* Worn down, browbeat for hours, fearing for his family, the situation must ha seemed hopeless. If the only way to get out of this me was to tell a story, even if it wasn't the true story, J agreed to make a second phone call to Jud McDonald's chambers informing the jurist that he w ready to talk.

McDONALD'S CHAMBERS

Lamb writes:

> "Following his arrival in chambers, Jackson informed McDonald that he had first been approached about participating in the World Series fix outside the Ansonia Hotel. Chick Gandil offered him $5,000, a sum rejected by Jackson as 'that wasn't enough to influence a laborer to do a dirty deed'."[87]

According to newspaper accounts, McDonald did so testify at the Black Sox trial in 1921.[88] I believe that the Judge was incorrect. It was Lefty, not Joe, who told the grand jury in 1920 that he was approached by Gandil outside the Ansonia Hotel and offered the $5,000. Lefty responded by saying, "That is not enough money for an ordinary working man to do a dirty trick."[89] Joe told the grand jury that he was first approached by Gandil in Boston either September 19 or 20 and, therefore, could not have attended the initial meeting of the crooked players at the Ansonia Hotel in New York City on either September 16 or 17. I do not believe Joe told McDonald that he was approached by Gandil in New York City and then, minutes later, told the grand jury that it was in Boston where Chick made the initial offer. I believe McDonald got the players confused at the 1921 trial and mistakenly indicated it was Joe rather than Lefty who was first offered a bribe by Gandil outside the Ansonia.

In his article, Lamb argues there is no "readily apparent reason for Judge McDonald to have testified falsely about Jackson's admission of fix complicity in chambers prior to his grand jury appearance when McDonald appeared as a witness in the Jackson civil trial (in 1924)."[90] I do not believe the Judge "testified falsely." What I do believe is after Joe's first telephone call to the Judge's chambers proclaiming his honesty and being told by McDonald that he knew he was not an honest man, Austrian continued browbeating him,

249

wearing him down and telling him that the truth would not be believed eventually convincing Joe that he must confess. Innocent people have confessed to much worse.

Thoroughly stressed out, feeling as if he could explode and in complete despair, the ballplayer did erupt at reporters after having flashbulbs go off in his face as he was being led to the grand jury room. Joe cursed his fate, cursed the gamblers and cursed baseball saying he wished he had never heard of the game, had never come North because he knew bad things would happen if he left his beloved South. And bad things did happen.

THE GRAND JURY

The two Joes testified. One admitted he had been a part of the plot while the other insisted he had always played to win, which was befuddling, I am sure, to anyone present in the grand jury room. But not befuddling enough for ASA Replogle to ask the slugger to explain the inherent contradictions in his testimony:

> REPLOGLE: How much did he (Gandil) promise you?
>
> JOE: $20,000 if I would take part.
>
> REPLOGLE: And you said you would?
>
> JOE: Yes, sir.[91]

But later:

> REPLOGLE: Did you make any intentional errors yourself that day?

> JOE: No, sir, not during the whole Series.

> REPLOGLE: Did you bat to win?

> JOE: Yes.

> REPLOGLE: And fielded the balls at the outfield to win?"

> JOE: I did.[92]

> REPLOGLE: Did you do anything to throw these games?

> JOE: No, sir…I didn't have an error or make no misplay…I tried to win all the time.[93]

Joe's supporters believe he was testifying truthfully when he claimed he always played to win and, as the result of Austrian's coaching, falsely when he said he agreed to take part. Naturally, Joe's detractors believe the reverse. Alan Dershowitz has written, "Jackson told two diametrically opposed stories, one confessing his guilt and the other protesting his innocence. Logic leads us to believe the first story was probably Austrian's, the second Jackson's."[94]

As indicated above, Joe made no mention of anything that might implicate Comiskey; that he went to th owner's hotel room prior to Game One to ask to b suspended; that he took the envelope with the $5,000 t Comiskey's office and had the door slammed in his face He did testify he "offered to come here last fall in th investigation."[95] Neither did he mention the Novembe 1919 exchange of letters.

BRIGHAM

Henry Brigham, the grand jury foreman, testified i 1924 that Joe "denied being in the conspiracy. Jackso said that he had given his best effort…he didn't adm that he threw the games…or any game…that he had trie to see Comiskey after the Series to tell what he knew,"[and "Jackson never confessed to any involvement in th fix at all."[97]

As someone who has sat on several juries, includin a month's stint as a grand juror, I feel Brigham' statements are very significant. From my firsthan experience, I know there is much more to analyzing th veracity of a witness than merely reading their testimon on a printed page. The demeanor of a witness; their bod language; their facial expressions; their eye movement the timbre and tone of their voice can say so much abou what the witness is trying to communicate and whether or not he or she is being truthful. Brigham was there and he believed Joe. He did not believe Jackson had confessed to anything.

What if Joe had mentioned the November 1919 exchange of letters between him and Comiskey when he offered to tell all that he knew, but got no response from the White Sox owner? At one point during his testimony, he seemed to be on the verge of telling more when he was asked:

> REPLOGLE: Didn't you think it was the right thing for you to go and tell Comiskey about it?
>
> JOE: I did tell them once.[98]

However, the ballplayer then shifts to talking about Gandil. It's as if he caught himself as he was about to implicate Comiskey. Further evidence, I believe, of how well he was coached. Brigham "admitted that the grand jury had made no investigation of Comiskey's conduct pertaining to the running down of rumors after the 1919 Series. He denied that the grand jury ever considered indicting Comiskey."[99] It's my feeling had they been aware of the exchange of letters, the grand jury may well have investigated Comiskey's conduct and the cover-up would have been exposed...and Shoeless Joe, not Comiskey, would now be in the Baseball Hall of Fame.

JOE'S CIVIL SUIT

Jackson must have felt exhilarated as he took t
witness stand during his civil trial in 1924 believing
finally was being given the opportunity to tell his side
the story. Suing Comiskey for breach of the three-ye
contract that he signed in February 1920 and claiming
should have been paid for the 1921 and '22 seasons, J
received rave reviews from the press for his performan
while being questioned by his attorney, Raymo
Cannon. However, the cheers turned to jeers when
faced cross examination by the White Sox counsel and
was revealed his testimony at the civil trial grea
differed from what he had said before the grand ju
The Judge cited him for contempt and had him jail
briefly declaring, "Either his testimony here or
testimony before the Chicago grand jury was false.
think the false testimony was given here."[100] Carr
writes, "When the grand jury material surfaced...a
when it was admitted into the trial, there was no sto
Jackson could tell that could not be contradicted by t
earlier testimony."[101] Is that really true?

One major part of Joe's testimony at the civil trial
I believe, corroborated by his grand jury testimony.
the 1924 trial, Joe stated Lefty came to his hotel roc
with $5,000 the night of the last game of the Series
October 9, 1919. He had testified previously before t
grand jury in 1920 that the bribe offer was made af
Game Four: 2

REPLOGLE: When was it that this money was brought to your room and that you talked to Mrs. Jackson?

JOE: It was the second trip to Cincinnati. That night we were leaving.

REPLOGLE: That was after the fourth game?

JOE: I believe it was, yes.[102]

Williams also initially testified before the grand jury that he gave the bribe money to Joe after Game Four.

WILLIAMS: Cicotte lost the next game (Four). The next night (no game was played that day) I was called over the telephone, I don't know whether by Gandil or whom, and told me there was a package for me…I went up. Gandil was there, and there was two packages there each containing $5,000…So I took the dough and got a taxicab and went to… Mr. Jackson…I threw one package on the bed…We went to Cincinnati (after Game Four) and came back.[103]

Referring to Joe's grand jury testimony, Lamb writes that, "On the evening before the White Sox were to return to Cincinnati for Game Five, Lefty Williams entered Jackson's room at the Lexington Hotel and threw $5,000 onto the bed."[104] As noted above, Jackson and

Williams both testified they went to Cincinnati after Game Four. However, this is not correct since Game Five was played in Chicago. The team did not return to Cincinnati until after Game Five. It's very interesting that both Jackson and Williams were mistaken about when they returned to Cincinnati which lends credence to the idea that they were coached by Austrian so their stories matched. Williams later said during his 1920 grand jury testimony that "after the first two games we were supposed to get our money, but I never got a nickle (sic) until the last two games were played (Games 7 and 8)."[105]

If true, as I believe it is, the testimony about the bribe offer being made after Game Four could not possibly be correct because Lefty had not yet received any money. Joe, therefore, appears to be telling the truth when he said during his 1924 civil trial that Williams brought the bribe to his hotel after Game Eight on October 9. When the pitcher offered him the envelope with the dirty money, Joe angrily told him that he was going to tell Comiskey about the bribe the next morning (October 10, 1919). That he went to Comiskey's office on that date is verified by his 1920 grand jury testimony:

> REPLOGLE: When was the last time you saw him and talked to him (Gandil)?

> JOE: It was on the following morning after the Series were over (October 10) that day in Comiskey's office, waiting in there.

REPLOGLE: What did you say to him at that time?

JOE: I told him there was a hell of a lot of scandal going around for what had happened. He said, "To hell with it." He was about half drunk. I went on out and left that night.[106]

According to Gropman, "Comiskey, whom we know from (team secretary) Harry's Diary was at that very moment hearing the details of the fix from two of the guilty players (Gandil and outfielder Happy Felsch), refused to see Jackson. 'Go home,' Grabiner said. 'We know what you want'…Jackson waited in the outer office for more than an hour, then left."[107] Lamb writes "immediately after the Series was lost, Comiskey informed Chick Gandil and Happy Felsch that he intended to have fix rumors investigated and that if any Sox players were found to be corrupt, he was 'going to put them out of business'."[108] So, it would appear Joe's claim that after being given the bribe money by Lefty, he went the next morning to Comiskey's office where he had an encounter with Gandil in the waiting room, was true. Joe's account appears to be verified by his 1920 grand jury testimony and by Harry's Diary. Why didn't Joe during his grand jury testimony mention the incriminating details about his attempting to show the owner the $5,000 and asking to talk to Comiskey about the Series? Again, I believe it was because he was well-coached by Austrian.   257

Jacob Pomrenke, during the Black Sox Scandal Centennial Symposium held in Chicago on September 28, 2019, said:

> "There are some reports, a little bit of evidence about Shoeless Joe Jackson possibly reporting the fix either before the World Series or after the World Series to either Kid Gleason or Charles Comiskey, but it's very thin evidence. It's something that Shoeless Joe only said many years later, but his story changed, and the details changed so it's very difficult to know for sure whether he told Gleason or Comiskey."[109]

I disagree with Pomrenke's comments that there is only "very thin evidence" that Jackson reported the fix or at least tried to after the World Series to Comiskey and "it's something that Shoeless Joe only said many years later and the details changed." It wasn't "many years later." Joe consistently testified he went to Comiskey's office the day after the Series ended on October 10, 1919 both during his 1920 grand jury testimony, the month the scandal broke, and at his 1924 civil trial. I believe this is solid evidence that corroborates the fact that he tried to report the fix to Comiskey. It is true that Joe did not mention asking Comiskey to suspend him before the start of the 1919 World Series until his 1949 *SPORT Magazine* interview but, as indicated above, I believe he was telling the truth because how else would he have known about the Fullerton/Comiskey meeting that took place in the owner's hotel room which Joe interrupted on the morning of Game One?

Obviously, Joe was poorly coached by his attorney, Cannon, during the 1924 civil trial because Cannon must have anticipated the White Sox defense was very likely to enter Joe's 1920 grand jury transcript into the record. Cannon, whom many considered to be the "best trial lawyer in Wisconsin"...having won 100 consecutive jury verdicts,[110] should have prepped Joe for the probability that he would be questioned about the contradictions between his two testimonies. Instead, Cannon is described as sitting "helplessly"[111] as Joe denied much of what he had said during his 1920 testimony. Lamb reports regarding the transcript of Jackson's 1920 grand jury testimony:

> "The transcript was not utilized during the Jackson deposition...(this) should not have lulled Jackson into a false sense of security about his risk of being confronted with his grand jury testimony."[112]

Joe's attorney also should not have been "lulled into a false sense of security," as he apparently was because as Lamb further writes: 259

"Nor was the Jackson side surprised by (Whi
Sox attorney) Hudnall's possession of
plaintiff's attorney Cannon having made
motion to preclude the transcript's use at the ci
trial. That motion was denied by Jud
Gregory."[113]

Joe was badly served both by Comiskey's attorne
Austrian, who represented his client impeccably prior
Jackson's grand jury testimony, and his apparen
overrated "star quality"[114] attorney Cannon during l
civil suit.

Comiskey appears to have testified falsely hims
when he was a witness at Joe's civil trial when
claimed "his suspicions about the 1919 World Ser
were initially aroused by (Chicago gambler) Mc
Tennes, who had telephoned him…on the morning
Game Two."[115] In a December 1930 intervie
however, the owner admitted he had learned of the fix
the morning of Game One. He also testified he "had i
been aware of Jackson's receipt of $5,000 from Le
Williams…If he had known…(he) would not have s
club secretary Grabiner to Georgia in February of 19
to sign Jackson to a new contract."[116] As noted abo
Joe said Grabiner told him when he signed the three-ye
contract in February 1920 that they were aware of
Williams bribe money.

Fullerton also appears not to have been telling the truth when he testified at the civil trial about "how he came to suspect a fix. Fullerton related that prior to Game One, he encountered old acquaintance Bill Burns, who advised the witness to 'wise up' about betting on the Chisox to win the 1919 Series. Burns assured him, 'The Reds are in.' But Fullerton had not taken Burns seriously and did not report any concern about Series integrity to Comiskey."[117] In direct contrast, "Years later—after Comiskey's death and the expiration of the statute of limitations on a false testimony charge—Fullerton had an entirely different story, writing that he had informed Comiskey before Game One of talk that the Series was fixed."[118]

THE BANK ACCOUNT

Regarding Joe's depositing the bribe money in a Georgia bank account, I believe it is significant that he waited almost two months before making the deposit. He had tried to show the $5,000 to Comiskey the day after receiving it and, I am also convinced, he would have brought it with him to Chicago if the owner had responded to his November 15, 1919 letter. Because he received no response, Joe decided in December that he may as well bank it. He testified at his '24 civil trial that he "didn't want the damn stuff (the $5000), and I thought just this way, since that lousy so-called gambling outfit had used my name, I might as well have their money as for him (Williams)."[119] Joe also testified, after asking Grabiner in February 1920 about the money, he was told "as long as that bunch of bums used your name, you did the only sensible thing in keeping it."[120] I believe Comiskey and his people wanted Joe to keep the money because he would then be implicated and less likely to expose the owner's cover-up.

COMISKEY A SCROOGE—MYTH OR FACT?

The Number one myth about the Black Sox scandal, according to SABR's "Eight Myths Out" project, is the idea White Sox owner Charles Comiskey was a "Scrooge." In fact, "organizational contract cards at the National Baseball Hall of Fame show that the White Sox's Opening Day payroll of $88,461 was more than $11,500 higher than that of the National League champion Reds, and several of the Black Sox players were among the highest-paid at their positions. If they did feel resentment at their salaries under the reserve-clause system, so did players from 15 other major-league teams. The scandal was much more complex than disgruntled players trying to get back at the big, bad boss."[121]

Jacob Pomrenke refers to "the faulty premise that White Sox owner Charles Comiskey underpaid and mistreated his players so badly that they were easily susceptible to the lures of wily gamblers who bribed them to fix the World Series."[122] Lamb writes "tales of Comiskey's cheapness are fictional"[123] and "the notion that Comiskey was tight-fisted...was invented by Black Sox defense attorneys in 1921, part of an ultimately successful strategy to deflect responsibility for Series corruption onto culprits other than those on trial."[124] According to Mark Dugo, "It is probably about time that we eliminate for all time the belief that White Sox owner Charles Comiskey was cheap and that led to the players revolting and ultimately throwing the Series."[125] Robert Bergeson contends "Comiskey's alleged tight-fistedness and the assertion he was mean-spirited have been largely refuted."[126]

Eddie Cicotte, however, in his 1920 grand jury testimony stated that at the Ansonia Hotel meeting held in September of 1919:

> "Either McMullin or Gandil started by saying that we were not getting a devil of a lot of money, and that it looked as though we could make a good thing if we threw the World Series to Cincinnati."[127]

Chick Gandil in his *Sports Illustrated* interview published September 17, 1956 described Comiskey as "a sarcastic, belittling man who was the tightest owner in baseball. If a player objected to his miserly terms, Comiskey told him: 'You can take it or leave it.' Under baseball's slave laws, what could a fellow do but take it?"[128] G.W. Axelson in his 1919 Comiskey biography mentions the owner's "penchant for sarcasm."[129] Gandil himself adds sarcastically "I recall only one act of generosity on Comiskey's part. After we won the World Series in '17, he splurged with a case of champagne."[130] Lamb, criticizing the champagne scene in the John Sayles film *Eight Men Out,* writes the source of the scene is "likely" the Gandil article which he describes as being "notoriously unreliable."[131] However, Fleitz notes Ring Lardner attended the celebration and remarked the champagne "tasted like stale piss."[132] While Pomrenke writes "stories about (Comiskey's) team playing in dirty laundry…are far-fetched, if not outright false,"[133] Gandil stated while "the White Sox in 1919 weren't a harmonious club…there was a common bond among most of us—our dislike for Comiskey…So help me, the fellow was tight. Many times we played in filthy uniforms because he was trying to keep down the cleaning tab."[134] It was reported at the trial in 1921 that the players were "forced to pay 50 cents to have their uniforms laundered."[135]

In SABR's own publications such as *Scandal on the Southside,* there are references to players' dissatisfaction with their wages. James R. Nitz writes Happy Felsch left the team "because of disputes with Comiskey over pay" while some of the White Sox particularly Lefty Williams were playing for "lower-than-market-salaries" and "the club was torn with dissension over wage disparities."[136] Nitz also writes Felsch, Jackson and Gandil "were rightly upset that their three salaries combined were less than the $15,000 made by college-educated Eddie Collins"[137] and Felsch expressed "great contempt for the penny-pinching Comiskey."[138]

Lamb writes given what Collins was being paid, White Sox salaries were "imbalanced...Lefty Williams, and, to a lesser extent, Joe Jackson and Chick Gandil, were paid less than their talents would have commanded had normal salary conditions prevailed in early 1919."[139] According to Fleitz, Comiskey " was one of the highest paid players in the 1880s. He was a mediocre hitter with a .259 lifetime batting average when he earned $6000 a year as first baseman and manager of the St. Louis Browns. Now, 30 years later, he was paying Joe Jackson, the greatest natural hitter in the game, the same amount,"[140] while telling the public that he was paying the slugger $10,000 per annum.[141] "Shoeless Joe Jackson should have been paid twice as much as (he was) making at the time."[142]

Sox pitcher Win Noyes described Comiskey as "skinflint" and said the owner and "not Shoeless J Jackson should have been banned from baseball."[143] T grandson of another White Sox pitcher, Lefty Sulliva reported he said "whatever happened to Comiske Comiskey deserved,"[144] and he felt "pure hate"[145] for t club owner. Sox outfielder Eddie Murphy "complain of petty things the owner did that annoyed his playe Murphy believed that Comiskey underpaid his playe and was rotten to them in other ways."[146] Swede Risbe complained about "Comiskey's starvation wages".[147]

Sox manager Kid Gleason had "quit baseball fo year because of a salary dispute with Comiskey." During the 1919 season when attendance was mu higher than expected, Gleason agreed to talk to the owr after the players threatened to revolt if their contra were not renegotiated.[149] Despite having been a memt of the Brotherhood of Professional Baseball Playe which was formed to protest the reserve clause and le salaries nearly 30 years before, Comiskey refused renegotiate.

Gene Carney opined, "Comiskey was probably i exceptionally tight. Every owner wielded the reser clause as the ultimate closer in contract negotiations." Baseball "was a legal monopoly, a business in whi players were in fact slaves...They were property." Fleitz asserts, "Comiskey was not a monster. Indeed,

Comiskey was a typical purveyor of the business ethics of the era. He made as much money for himself as he could and spent as little of it on his employees as he could possibly get away with spending."[152] According to Hornbaker, "Across the major leagues, a wider and wider divide grew between players and club owners…Comiskey was…going to wear the same badge his fellow owners wore: being labeled a penny-pincher and cheap…owners were tagged as being greedy, and Comiskey was lumped into the pile."[153]

Hornbaker also states that "the divide between club management and the players… wasn't limited to any one league city."[154] Management was criticized "as being tightfisted and obsessively greedy."[155] "The sentiment of major leaguers with regard to the supposed greed of club owners was one of the most common threads across the sport. Those who bought into the idea felt magnates were in a place to rack up incredible sums of money off their hard work, and believed they continuously received the short end of the stick during salary negotiations. 'Leave it to the big bosses to cop all the dough,' an unnamed member of the Sox told a reporter …(Comiskey), like other big league moguls, (was) perceived for their insatiability for wealth."[156]

The players throughout the major leagues threatened to strike after the 1916 season when the owners "wanted to rework contracts to ensure the 10-day clause was an available option as well as strengthening the reserve clause."[157] The Federal League, which went out of business after the 1915 season, had given the players a taste of what they could earn on an open market as free agents were it not for the reserve clause.

According to Paul Browne, "Bob Hoie makes a convincing argument that the White Sox of 1919 were not underpaid in comparison to other players around the American League. But that doesn't necessarily mean that they didn't *feel* underpaid."[158] Hornbaker writes the salaries of ballplayers were "rarely given out by people in the know, seldom confirmed and hardly ever correct.' The salaries were often "overinflated" by pundits.[159] So it is possible the White Sox perceived they were underpaid because they did not apparently know what other players were making and may well have believed the reported inflated salaries. Oftentimes, perception is more important than reality.

CONCLUSION

The great hitter Ted Williams fought ferociously for years to have Joe reinstated into organized baseball so he might take his rightful place in the Hall of Fame. Explaining why he was so passionate about the subject Williams said he loved "this game so much that I can't believe baseball would have done anything wrong...But maybe, in Jackson's case...it has done something unfair."[160]

As great an all-time hitter as Williams was--and such luminaries as Cobb, Ruth, Gehrig and Wagner were, and such current stars as Cabrera, Pujols and Trout are--I still think Shoeless Joe might have been recognized as the greatest of them all were it not for the scandal. He hit a combined .367 over what proved to be his final two seasons including .382 in 1920 which was the first year of the live-ball era. He may well have, if he had continued to play, lifted his lifetime batting average over .360 thus challenging Ty Cobb for the highest batting average in the history of the game.

Joe said during his 1949 *Sport Magazine* interview that no one asked him, when he emerged from the courthouse after testifying before the grand jury, to "Say it ain't so, Joe!" If anyone had asked, however, the ballplayer stated, "Oh, I would have said it ain't so, all right."[161] And so do we, who are proud to call ourselves Shoeless Joe Jackson admirers, insist on saying to all who listen: IT AIN'T SO!

END NOTES

[1] Bill Lamb, "An Ever-Changing Story" *SABR Baseball Research Journal Spring 2019,* p. 45.

[2] Ibid., p. 37.

[3] Tim Hornbaker, *Fall From Grace* (New York, NY: Sports Publishing, 2018) p. 172.

[4] Ibid., p. 115.

[5] Ibid., p. 175.

[6] Ibid., p. 172.

[7] *Greenville News,* July 28, 1946, p. 12.

[8] Tim Hornbaker, *Fall from Grace,* p. 172.

[9] Ibid., p. 172.

[10] Ibid., p. 172.

[11] William F. Lamb, *Black Sox in the Courtroom* (Jefferson NC: McFarland & Co., Inc., 2013) p. 175.

[12] *Baltimore Sun,* August 2, 1998, p. 74.

[13] Gene Carney, *Burying the Black Sox* (Washington, DC: Potomac Books, Inc., 2006) p. 175.

[14] William F. Lamb, *Black Sox in the Courtroom,* p. 174.

[15] Ibid., p. 174

[16] David L. Fleitz, *Shoeless: The Life and Times of Joe Jackson* (Jefferson NC: McFarland & Co., 2001) p. 277.

[17] William R. Herzog II, "From Scapegoat to Icon", *The Faith of 50 Million* (Louisville KY: Westminster John Knox Press, 2002) p. 101.

[18] William F. Lamb, *Black Sox in the Courtroom,* p. 50.

[19] William R. Herzog II, "From Scapegoat to Icon", *The Faith of 50 Million,* p. 101.

[20] William F. Lamb, *Black Sox in the Courtroom,* p. 156.

[21] Bill Lamb, "An Ever-Changing Story", p. 45.

[22] William F. Lamb, *Black Sox in the Courtroom,* p. 179.

[23] Donald Gropman, *Say it Ain't So, Joe!* (New York, NY: Carol Publishing Group, 1995.) p. 226.

[24] *Pittsburgh Daily News,* September 30, 1920, p. 8.

[25] David L. Fleitz, *Shoeless: The Life and Times of Joe Jackson,* p. 279.

[26] Tim Hornbaker, *Turning the Black Sox White* (New York, NY: Sports Publishing, 2014) p. 329,

[27] Tim Hornbaker, *Fall from Grace,* p. 96.

[28] "Listen to Highlights from Eight Myths Out Events", *SABR Black Sox Scandal Research Committee Newsletter,* v. 11, no. 2, p. 10.

[29] J.M. Flagler, "Requiem for a Southpaw", *The New Yorker* 12-? 59, p. 230.

[30] J.M. Flagler obituary *NY Times* September 28, 1972 p. 50.

[31] William F. Lamb, *Black Sox in the Courtroom,* p. 49.

[32] Charles Fountain, *The Betrayal* (Oxford, London: Oxford University Press, 2016) p. 141.

[33] Gene Carney, *Burying the Black Sox,* p. 331.

[34] Ibid., p. 337.

[35] Donald Gropman, *Say it Ain't So, Joe!* p. 278.

[36] Ibid., p. 279.

[37] Ibid., p. 270.

[38] Gene Carney, *Burying the Black Sox,* p. 177.

[39] William R. Herzog II, "From Scapegoat to Icon", *The Faith of 50 Million,* p. 111.

[40] Furman Bisher, "This is the Truth!" *Sport Magazine* 1949 (internet) p. 2.

[41] Bill Lamb, "An Ever-Changing Story", p. 44.

[42] Hugh Fullerton, "I Recall", *The Sporting News* October 17, 19? (internet) p. 3.

[43] Jacob Pomrenke, "New Comiskey Interview May Lend Credence to Fullerton Claim", *SABR Black Sox Scandal Researc? Committee Newsletter,* vol. 9 no. 2, December 2017, p. 13.

[44] Hugh Fullerton, "I Recall" (internet) p. 4.

[45] William F. Lamb, *Black Sox in the Courtroom,* p. 134.

[46] Ibid., p. 6.

[47] Charles Fountain, *The Betrayal,* p. 149.

[48] William R. Herzog II, "From Scapegoat to Icon", *The Faith of 50 Million,* p. 100.

[49] Ibid., p. 100.

[50] Bill Lamb, "An Ever-Changing Story", p. 37.

[51] William F. Lamb, *Black Sox in the Courtroom,* p. 56.

[52] Bill Lamb, "An Ever-Changing Story", p. 44

[53] Ibid., p. 45.

[54] *Chicago Tribune,* September 29, 1920, p. 2.

[55] "Listen to Highlights from Eight Myths Out Events", *SABR Black Sox Scandal Research Committee Newsletter,* vol. 11 no. 2 p. 10.

[56] Bill Lamb, "An Ever-Changing Story", p. 45.

[57] Harvey Frommer, *Shoeless Joe and Ragtime Baseball* (Dallas, Texas: Taylor Publishing Co., 1992) p. 201.

[58] William F. Lamb, *Black Sox in the Courtroom,* p. 63.

[59] Charles Fountain, *The Betrayal,* pp. 167-68.

[60] Gene Carney, *Burying the Black Sox,* p. 166.

[61] Bill Lamb, "An Ever-Changing Story", p. 46.

[62] William R. Herzog, "From Scapegoat to Icon", *The Faith of 50 Million,* p. 129.

[63] Bill Lamb, "Alfred Austrian" *SABR* (internet) p. 2.

[64] Ibid., p. 3.

[65] Bill Lamb, "An Ever-Changing Story", p. 44.

[66] William F. Lamb, *Black Sox in the Courtroom,* p. 73.

[67] Bill Lamb, "Alfred Austrian" *SABR* (internet) p. 5.

[68] Charles Fountain, *The Betrayal,* pp. 124-26.

[69] Bill Lamb, "Alfred S. Austrian, White Sox Corporate Counsel", *SABR Black Sox Scandal Research Committee Newsletter,* vol. 11 no. 1, p. 10.

[70] Tim Hornbaker, *Fall from Grace,* p. 157.

[71] Ibid., p. 157.

[72] William R. Herzog II, "From Scapegoat to Icon", *The Faith of 50 Million,* p. 120.

[73] Bill Lamb, "An Ever-Changing Story", p. 44.

[74] Ibid., p. 45.

[75] Bill Lamb, "Alfred Austrian" *SABR* (internet) p. 5.

[76] Charles Fountain, *The Betrayal,* p. 156.

[77] Harvey Frommer, *Shoeless Joe and Ragtime Baseball,* p. 201.

[78] William R. Herzog II, "From Scapegoat to Icon", *The Faith of 50 Million,* p. 117.

[79] Bill Lamb, "An Ever-Changing Story", p. 38.

[80] David L. Fleitz, *Shoeless: The Life and Times of Joe Jackson,* p. 224.

[81] Bill Lamb, "An Ever-Changing Story", p. 45.

[82] Ibid., p. 45.

[83] Saul Kassin, "False Confessions: How Innocent People Confess to Crimes in America" (internet) p. 2.

[84] Gene Carney, *Burying the Black Sox,* p.123.

[85] Charles Fountain, *The Betrayal,* p. 164.

[86] Bill Veeck, "Harry's Diary", *The Hustler's Handbook,* p. 270.

[87] William F. Lamb, *Black Sox in the Courtroom,* p. 122.

[88] *Chicago Tribune,* July 26, 1921, p. 3.

[89] Lefty Williams, 1920 grand jury testimony transcript, Chicago History Museum, Black Sox Scandal Collection, p. 26.

[90] Bill Lamb, "An Ever-Changing Story", p. 45.

[91] Harvey Frommer, *Shoeless Joe and Ragtime Baseball,* p. 195.

[92] Ibid., p.200.

[93] Ibid., p. 202.

[94] Donald Gropman, *Say It Ain't So, Joe!",* xix.

[95] Harvey Frommer, *Shoeless Joe and Ragtime Baseball,* p. 201.

[96] Gene Carney, *Burying the Black Sox,* p. 176.

[97] Donald Gropman, *Say It Ain't So, Joe!* p. 196.

[98] Harvey Frommer, *Shoeless Joe and Ragtime Baseball,* p. 199.

[99] Gene Carney, *Burying the Black Sox,* p. 176.

[100] William F. Lamb, *Black Sox in the Courtroom,* p. 187.

[101] Gene Carney, *Burying the Black Sox,* p. 3.

[102] Harvey Frommer, *Shoeless Joe and Ragtime Baseball,* p. 194.

[103] Lefty Williams 1920 grand jury testimony transcript, Chicago History Museum Black Sox Scandal Collection, p. 27.

[104] Bill Lamb, "An Ever-Changing Story", p. 39.

[105] Lefty Williams 1920 grand jury testimony transcript Chicago History Museum Black Sox Scandal Collection, p. 36.

[106] Harvey Frommer, *Shoeless Joe and Ragtime Baseball,* p. 203.

[107] Donald Gropman, *Say It Ain't So, Joe!,* p. 172.

[108] William F. Lamb, *Black Sox in the Courtroom,* p. 174.

[109] "Listen to Symposium Highlights" *SABR Black Sox Scandal Research Committee Newsletter* December 2019 v. 11 no. 2, p. 5.

[110] William F. Lamb, *Black Sox in the Courtroom,* p. 166.

[111] Bill Lamb, "An Ever-Changing Story", p. 42.

[112] William F. Lamb, *Black Sox in the Courtroom,* p. 172.

[113] Bill Lamb, "An Ever-Changing Story", p. 47.

[114] William F. Lamb, *Black Sox in the Courtroom,* p. 166.

[115] Ibid., p. 173.

[116] Ibid., p. 174.

[117] Ibid., pp. 179-80.

[118] Ibid., p. 182.

[119] Gene Carney, *Burying the Black Sox,* p. 73.

[120] *New York Times,* January 31, 1924, p. 8.

[121] "Eight Myths Out", *SABR Black Sox Scandal Research Committee (*internet)

[122] Jacob Pomrenke, "Revisiting the Eight Myths Out", *SABR*

Black Sox Scandal Research Committee Newsletter, vol. 10 no. 2, p. 3.

[123] Bill Lamb, "Alfred Austrian" *SABR* (internet) p. 1.

[124] Bill Lamb, "Based on a True Story: Eliot Asinof, John Sayles and the Fictionalization of the Black Sox Scandal," *The Inside Game, The Official Newsletter of SABR'S Deadball Era Committee,* v. XIX no.3, p. 36.

[125] Mark Dugo, "The Betrayal: The 1919 World Series and the Birth of Modern Baseball (review)" *The Inside Game, The Official Newsletter of SABR'S Deadball Era Committee,* vol. XIX no. 3 p. 31.

[126] Robert Bergeson, "Did 'just cause' exist for Buck's punishment?" *SABR Black Sox Scandal Research Committee Newsletter,* v. 11 no. 2, p. 13.

[127] Eddie Cicotte 1920 grand jury testimony, Chicago History Museum Black Sox Scandal Collection. p. 1.

[128] Arnold Gandil, "My Story" *Sports Illustrated* (internet) p. 3.

[129] "Axelson's 1919 Book 'Commy' Available Online", *SABR Black Sox Scandal Research Committee Newsletter,* v. 4 no. 1, p. 11.

[130] Arnold Gandil, "My Story" *Sports Illustrated* (internet) p. 3.

[131] Bill Lamb, "Based on a True Story: Eliot Asinof, John Sayles and the Fictionalization of the Black Sox Scandal", *The Inside Game, The Official Newsletter of SABR'S Deadball Era Committee,* v. XIX no. 3, p. 40.

[132] David L. Fleitz, *Shoeless: The Life and Times of Joe Jackson,* p. 146.

[133] Jacob Pomrenke, "Revisiting Eight Myths Out" *SABR Black Sox Scandal Research Committee Newsletter,* v. 10 no. 2, p. 3.

[134] Arnold Gandil, "My Story" (internet) p. 3.

[135] Tim Hornbaker, *Fall from Grace,* p. 194.

[136] James Nitz, "Happy Felsch", *SABR Scandal on the Southside* (Phoenix, AZ: Society for American Baseball Research, Inc., 2015) p. 55.

[137] Ibid., p. 56.

[138] Ibid., p. 64.

[139] William F. Lamb, *Black Sox in the Courtroom,* p. 7.

[140] David Fleitz, *Shoeless: The Life and Times of Joe Jackson,* p. 160.

[141] Charles Fountain, *The Betrayal,* p. 221.

[142] David L. Fleitz, *Shoeless: The Life and Times of Joe Jackson,* p. 161.

[143] Bruce Allardice, "Win Noyes", *SABR Scandal on the Southside,* p. 164.

[144] Jacob Pomrenke, "Lefty Sullivan" *Scandal on the Southside,* p. 209.

[145] Ibid., p. 210.

[146] Paul Browne, "A Grandfather's Tale: Interviewing Eddie Murphy III", *SABR Black Sox Scandal Research Committee Newsletter,* v. 7 no. 1, p. 13.

[147] "Sign for the Tip Money Comiskey Offered? Never!"—Swede Risberg. *SABR Black Sox Scandal Research Committee Newsletter,* v. 12 no. 1 p. 24.

[148] Gene Carney, *Burying the Black Sox,* p. 277.

[149] "Baseball History in 1919. Say it ain't so!" (internet) p. 2.

[150] Gene Carney, *Burying the Black Sox,* p. 195.

[151] Ibid., p. 156.

[152] David L. Fleitz, *Shoeless: The Life and Times of Joe Jackson,* p. 109.

[153] Tim Hornbaker, *Turning the Black Sox White,* p. 211.

[154] Tim Hornbaker, *Fall from Grace,* p. 96.

[155] Ibid., p. 130.

[156] Ibid., p. 83.

[157] Ibid., pp. 95-96.

[158] Paul Browne, "A Grandfather's Tale: Interviewing Eddie Murphy III", *SABR Black Sox Scandal Research Committee Newsletter,* v. 7 no. 1, p. 13.

[159] Tim Hornbaker, *Fall from Grace,* p. 57.

[160] *Chicago Tribune,* "Jackson may have been Shoeless but not Hopeless", 3/1/98 (internet)

[161] Furman Bisher. "This is the Truth!", *SPORT Magazine* 1949 (internet) p. 3.